Being There

Being There

The Parables in a Different Voice

"Come and See"
—JOHN 1:39

William J. O'Malley, SJ

ORBIS BOOKS
Maryknoll, New York 10545

ORBIS BOOKS
Maryknoll, New York 10545

Fathers and Brothers
MARYKNOLL™
TOGETHER IN GOD'S MISSION OF MERCY

Founded in 1970, Orbis Books endeavors to publish works that en-lighten the mind, nourish the spirit, and challenge the conscience. The publishing arm of the Maryknoll Fathers and Brothers, Orbis seeks to explore the global dimensions of the Christian faith and mission, to invite dialogue with diverse cultures and religious tra-ditions, and to serve the cause of reconciliation and peace. The books published reflect the views of their authors and do not represent the official position of the Maryknoll Society. To learn more about Maryknoll and Orbis Books, please visit our website at www.maryknollsociety.org.

Published by Orbis Books, Box 302, Maryknoll, NY 10545-0302.

Queries regarding rights and permissions should be addressed to: Orbis Books, P.O. Box 302, Maryknoll, NY 10545-0302.

Manufactured in the United States of America.

Manuscript editing and typesetting by Joan Weber Laflamme.

Library of Congress Cataloging-in-Publication Data

Names: O'Malley, William J.
Title: Being there : the parables of Jesus in a different voice / Wil-liam J.
  O'Malley, S.J.
Description: Maryknoll : Orbis Books, 2016.
Identifiers: LCCN 2015040762 | ISBN 9781626981812 (pbk.)
Subjects: LCSH: Jesus Christ—Parables.
Classification: LCC BT375.3 .O56 2016 | DDC 226.8/06—dc23
LC record available at http://lccn.loc.gov/2015040762

For Ehtesham Rehmani

Contents

Introduction

*A*nyone past tenth grade knows a parabola is a curve. Fewer have been told that each of Jesus's parables is also a curve, in fact, a curve ball (Greek: *para-* "around," *ballein-* "to throw"). The pitcher grips the ball across the seams at the widest part, which causes the pitch to drop as it gets close to home plate. The batter sees the ball coming at a certain level, swings— and it's not there. The batter realizes he or she has been snookered. Parables do that.

Jesus gets the *listeners* to answer exactly what he would have said if they hadn't had their vigilant preconceptions up. The clearest example is the Good Samaritan. The reader or listener misses a lot of what Jesus intended just taking the story in isolation from the occasion that provoked it. A whole new dimension arises in including the inquirer who gave rise to the parable and whose attitude checked Jesus from answering him flat out. The questioner was "a doctor of the Law," a lifetime scholar, approved not only by his demanding expert teachers but sealed with Temple blessing: "validly ordained." He's not only an "official," which makes him automatically self-important, but— worse—the guy we all hated in school who could find flaws even in the teacher's arguments. What's more, this man, bristling with expertise, comes to Jesus—who is only a layman, remember—asking *his* advice. In this expert's mind Jesus has no further academic authentication than the limits of the Nazareth rabbi who instructed him. And he's not asking just a clarification about practice like healing on the Sabbath or paying Roman taxes. He's asking *the* question: In the eyes of

God, what do human beings need to do to fulfill their purpose—to feel they justify God's gift of existence? What's the innermost kernel of God's will?

Like any good teacher, Jesus turns the question back on him. "You're the expert. What's written in the Law?" The lawyer gives the only answer he can: "Love God, love your neighbor." And Jesus answers, "Perfect. Do that, and you'll do just fine. Next?" But the lawyer is just getting started. Like a skilled debater, he concedes in order to creep back and dominate. He hasn't gotten to his *real* question: the trap. "But then, sir, who *is* my neighbor?"

The unstated ambush question—his *real* question—is this: Whom can I *exclude*?

Pharisees readily excluded non-Pharisees, which surely simplified conscience matters, since it effectively eliminated nearly everybody on earth. But Jewish lawyers fine tuned it more exquisitely, excluding all heathen pagans; those considered "unclean"—from certified lepers to women just after childbirth; anyone of a different race; all the marginalized like beggars, prostitutes, and tax collectors.

If Jesus had come out and declared his answer forthrightly, "Your neighbor is *any* human being—*especially* those you find repellent," the lawyer would have flared his skirts and gone smugly on his way. Instead, shrewd Jesus tells a story of a man battered and left by the road, ignored by "officially worthy" Jews and helped by a man who was himself a reject, a renegade Samaritan. And Jesus, all dewy-eyed innocence, completely upends the lawyer's question from "Whom must I treat as a neighbor" to "Who proved to *be* a neighbor?" And given the setup of the parable, there is simply only one possible answer. The kind man. Snookered. Checkmate.

As any teacher will testify, an even deeper resistance to learning comes not from antagonism but from complete indifference. Any teacher must ignite *curiosity*. Without that, the best a teacher can hope for is well-mannered tolerance.

Since the caves, the wiser men and women of the tribe have used stories to intrigue people to reassess their lives and to help children on the mystifying quest for adulthood. The concrete specifics of the story not only snag interest but also lay hold of the airy lesson or moral or understanding from way up there in ungraspable abstraction and bringing it down into here-and-now practical reality. Parables are wonders of incarnation.

There's a real connection—at least an analogy—between the "catch" in parables and in jokes. Something in both jerks us up, teases the mind to think further. For instance, a *New Yorker* cartoon showed a stuffy-looking guy sauntering past a porch with a sign reading "Beware the Dog!" But on the porch is this wildly grinning, tail-thrumming dog holding a sign saying, "Jesus loves you!" I laughed aloud. Why? It hooked me because it was so ridiculous, unexpected, silly—just like "It's as easy for a world-beater to get into the kingdom as for a fat-humped camel to herniate itself through the eye of a needle." But I've heard the needle joke too often, starting from long before I was old enough to appreciate wit.

For those reasons the parables are the most reliable source of the bedrock tradition; they're easy to remember. But always keep in mind that although Jesus had a sharp eye and skill with logic, he clearly was a poet, not an analyst. He explained with metaphors and stories that demanded the listener's (and reader's) cooperation.

The parables are concrete, held together by a co-
herent story line. They use stock devices still common
today: three servants with talents, priest-Levite-Samari-
tan, just like "a priest, a minister, and a rabbi walk into
a bar." In assembling material as editors the evangelists
used "hooks" linking ideas to similar situations and
even words, like a stand-up comic (lost coin, lost lamb,
lost son). That also holds for allusions back to Hebrew
scripture, which was their only book, using those links
as a confirmation of the consistent ways of the Yahweh
whom Jesus now called Abba.

Therefore, the insights embedded in stories were
more likely to be handed down in close to original for-
mulation. However, the gospel writers themselves used
them creatively, linking gospel events and doctrines to
later situations their new audiences faced, like persecution by both their Jewish former fellow believers and
pagan Roman society. Also, contemporary puzzlement
over the delay of what they had been led to believe
would be an impending end of the world tweaked
their presentation of previous acts and declarations.
Further, their audiences faced a quite new realization of
the difference between a real-but-not-literal kingdom
(the Christian community) in this world and a future
kingdom of God in heavenly fulfillment.

The gospel writers were applying the principles of
Jesus to new questions; the church has been doing the
same for the last twenty centuries.

But the results—the Gospels themselves, especially
the parables—suggest the gospel writers and the first
audiences were more adept and more comfortable
than many modern Christians with associative, rela-
tional understanding, the different right-brain skills
that spin out stories, poems, metaphors. Not the skills
that keep ledgers, but those that sell automobiles and

deodorants. They interlinked ideas and understandings more by means of "felt connections" and resonances from the Hebrew scriptures than by using the logical linkages a classroom teacher uses. Their work was not information or even the further stage of theologizing. Their ultimate motive was conversion.

Writers and listeners, then, were adept at the same gut feelings that *amplify* a technically trained doctor's rational insight, allowing a caring physician to go beyond empirical *causes* and help a patient contend with the psychological anguish of grasping for *reasons* to keep going. This is the same way grandmothers "know" a squalling grandchild is thirsty not croupy, the same intuitive skill musicians use when they shift pitches and rhythm midway through a tune simply because it "feels right." Art historians can spin out volumes of explanatory influences, but few can produce anything like the Sistine Chapel ceiling or force feed into a barbarian the awe it produces.

In *To Kill a Mockingbird* Atticus Finch tells his daughter: "If you just learn a single trick, Scout, you'll get along a lot better with all kinds of folks. You never really understand a person until you consider things from his point of view . . . until you climb inside of his skin and walk around in it."

We're not limiting ourselves here to just a "moral" or a "lesson" we could write down in a book—as Aesop did at the end of each of his fables—or the kind of principles of moral behavior painted on the walls of Oliver Twist's orphanage to keep pounding home discipline. But a story can manipulate, open up, form the reader's *attitude*, his or her point of view and expectations of life. Better than hand-me-down rules, stories offer a *felt understanding* of what it costs to be a decent human being. A reader can get inside the skin of Holden Caulfield and Hester Prynne, walk step by step with them through their painful experiences, and then come out of those borrowed lives *with* their deeper understanding of human life but *without* their scars.

Jesus seems to have intended his parables not for scholarly analysis but for meditation.

Interpretation

*R*eading what the *author* intended takes skill and effort. And humility. The author wants the reader to get a meaning beyond and richer than the literal story, but there is always the danger that an incautious reader will take one or two clues and run wild with them. For instance, when I first began to teach English, I gave juniors this simple poem:

> Greatly shining,
> The Autumn moon floats in the thin
>   sky;
> And the fish-ponds shake their backs
>   and flash their dragon scales
> As she passes over them.
>
> —AMY LOWELL (1874–1925)

Just a simple picture of the moon in a cloudless sky, reflected off ponds whose wavelets catch the light and make them look like dragon scales. No evidence of a hidden meaning.

One boy put up his hand: "I have a different interpretation."

"Okay, as long as evidence *in* the poem justifies it. It's not a Rorschach test: What does this make me think of?"

"I think it's about a U-2 [spy plane] flight over Red China."

We were all stunned.

"Where's your evidence?"

"Right there at the bottom: 'dragon scales.'"

"But . . . but you've just taken two words and spun out your own poem. Like putting a moustache on the Mona Lisa."

"That's *your* opinion."

"Why couldn't it be a U-2 flight over medieval England. Apparently they had dragons."

"That's your opinion. My opinion's as good as anybody else's."

I *had* him! "Look at the bottom. '1874–1925'! She was *dead*! There *was* no Red China! There were *no* U-2s!"

He was unfazed.

"That's *your* opinion."

There are limits imposed on legitimate interpretations of any segment of the Gospels, especially the parables. *Eisegesis* means reading *into* a segment a meaning that the evidence can't sustain, like the U-2 flight. For instance, the references to the coming end in the God-inspired Gospels impelled some to see the Hiroshima bomb as the first blow of the final battle, and AIDS as the plague that signals the end, and made Hale-Bopp Comet fanatics certain the end was hurtling toward us. Many early Christians assumed the end would come in their lives. It didn't.

Exegesis means reading *out* from. It demands all interpretations to be validated by evidence *in the text*. Which means it's very, very shaky to impose a meaning on the text that simply could not have been the intention of Jesus or the first-century Christian writers trying to communicate to *their* audiences.

Raymond Brown, SS, writes in *The Jerome Biblical Commentary*:

> Because Scripture is inspired and presumably this inspiration was for the good of all, there has arisen the fallacy that everyone should be able to pick up the Bible and read it profitably. If this implies that everyone should be able to find out what the sacred author is saying without preparation or study, it really demands of God in each instance a miraculous dispensation from the limitations imposed by differences of time and circumstance.

The primary task of the scriptural authors was to be intelligible *to their own times*. To read the Bible as the authors *intended* requires that our biblical education be proportionate to our other education. No one would dump *King Lear* on adolescents without a welter of notes, yet we blithely dump Luke on them and expect them to fathom it. Just because people know how to read does not guarantee they can read either Shakespeare or scripture with anything more than the vaguest comprehension.

Four Authors, Four Cultures

Jesus spoke to a different culture from ours—one in which, for instance, farmers sowed seed and *then* plowed, where there were two different ways of designating time, Roman and Hebrew, and where Italians planted mustard bushes and Palestinians did not. Also, four different personalities gathered the Jesus stories and edited them for different audiences. Mark was probably earliest, and Matthew and Luke wrote later editions of his book with new sources and insights. John is in a school by himself, more otherworldly, emphasizing a much "larger picture" than just everyday life in first-century Palestine. Mark is down to earth, rapid fire; Matthew, likely a teacher of the law himself, is hardest on the Jews; Luke is the gentlest, the only one with the parables of the Good Samaritan, the Prodigal Son, the Good Thief; John is poetical and strongly mystical.

Think of the difference in *tone* between Tennessee Williams and Earnest Hemingway—or more delicately between the tone of Williams and Flannery O'Connor. You get a different "sense" of a scene if the writer refers to cornmeal as grits rather than polenta. Moreover, a writer's intrusion of a striking concrete detail argues that it was worth remembering; for example, in John 27, Peter puts *on* clothes to jump from the boat to hurry to Jesus. That bit of a crude man's sense of decorum says a lot worth *remembering*. Some of the parables—Wheat and Weeds, the Rich Fool, the Good Samaritan—are so vivid it's quite possible Jesus took an actual recent event as a starting point. Scholars of Middle Eastern literature show that Jesus wasn't above borrowing common stories from other cultures—just as Shakespeare did. (The church did the same with Aristotle.) Writing for a sophisticated Gentile audience, Luke uses building techniques, court procedure, farming, and scenery familiar to his "European" readers. Similarly, Mark divides the segments of the night by the Roman not the Palestinian customs. The evangelists' differing uses of the Roman vs. the Palestinian divisions of the year cause a devil of a time trying to nail down the dates of Christmas and Easter.

Countless Retranslations

*T*here are also changes of meaning and emphasis simply in the transformation from one language to another. Jesus spoke Galilean Aramaic. Translating his words—especially household words—into the language and customs of a Greek culture took some approximations. Even in our own time translations of gospel Greek have caused incalculable spiritual pain. For instance, translating the Greek *teleios* as "perfect" and giving it the English connotations of "flawless" has caused many good souls to believe God expects them to be as unblemished as God himself, which is first-class blasphemy. What Jesus meant was "heading in the direction you were born for."

The message moved from Aramaic to Greek, from Greek to Latin, from Latin to the languages of Europe, and then into the Babel of languages around the world today. Just consider the subtle tonal, attitudinal difference even in three English translations of exactly the same Greek for Mary's hymn "The Magnificat":

> *King James (KJV):* And Mary said, "My soul doth magnify the Lord,
>> And my spirit hath rejoiced in God my Saviour."

> *Good News (GNT):* Mary said, "My heart praises the Lord;
>> my soul is glad because of God my Savior."

> *The Message (MSG):* And Mary said, "I'm bursting with God-news;
>> I'm dancing the song of my Savior God."

Embellishment

A word about the ancient Eastern storytellers' delight in embellishing numbers—just as later writers would fantasize dragons who drank whole lakes at a time and imagine Paul Bunyan eight feet tall (Goliath was 9'9"). Methuselah lived to be 969; Abram and Sarai had a child in their nineties; Noah lived 350 years after the Flood and died at the age of 950; Moses, according to some, was 120.

The same is true of the parables. The money entrusted in the Parable of the Talents was beyond computation. The amount—ten thousand talents—belies the fact that the yearly Roman tribute from the provinces of Galilee and Perea was two hundred talents. In the metaphor of the kingdom as yeast (Mt 13; Lk 13), the amount of flour would have fed a whole village. Supposing each man at the feeding of the five thousand had brought one wife and a minimum of three kids, Jesus fed not five thousand but closer to twenty-five thousand. Suffice it to say "there were a *lot*." It's beyond comprehension that a single grain of wheat could reproduce itself "a hundredfold" (Mk 4), or that, by sheer coincidence, every single invitee to a great banquet (Mt 22; Lk 14) would find a reason to beg off. *Unless* (for which there is no more evidence than a hunch) the host was a major mafioso, and they wouldn't dare be caught there by the tabloid paparazzi!

We also can't forget that the great Stephen Hawking has postulated black holes that can gobble up planets like peanuts. And also, beyond our already staggeringly huge universe, he suggests that this could be only a single universe in an infinite *series* of universes. The fact we know the Road Runner isn't really dead doesn't ruin the fun, does it?

It's called *willing suspension of disbelief.* To get hung up on such extravagance is to miss the whole point. Most police might draw their weapons two or three times in their a career, but no one complains that most TV cop shows expend more ammunition in a month than the War of 1812. And we readily forget we're not actually inside a courtroom but in our living rooms watching pixels popping on a screen.

It is difficult for ordinary Christians today to imagine the extent to which the presence of otherworldly realities permeated the lives of Christians in the Middle Ages and Hebrews in the time of Jesus. God mattered not just on Sabbath but every day. The extraordinary lived *within* the ordinary—villages, farms—growing "forever" in the "now."

Moreover, without the help of an expert commentator, it's almost impossible to tell whether the original intention of Jesus—speaking to a specific audience—meant that particular lesson was for ordinary people or for the Jewish hierarchy or for his own "seminarians." Nor can the ordinary reader tell without help whether the so-called watchfulness parables (speaking of unfaithful servants, a watchman, a thief in the night, bridesmaids) are exhorting the ordinary conscience to be prepared every single moment for the natural death that awaits us all, the earliest communities to be ever aware of unexpected death for their faith in the arena, speaking of the literal end of centralized Judaism when the Temple was destroyed in 70 CE, or even referring to the literal end of the whole world.

You can get a lot more from *King Lear* if you've read all the footnotes before you see a performance. Doing so is helpful. As long as you realize that the original story was intended for a response richer and more profound than mere intellectual enlightenment. The refined skills and insights of scholarly experts are the backbone of this book. But the ordinary, generally educated reader would find even experts' more popularized books presume more expertise than a long-ago college course. They seem to pick their way through scripture as if asking Jackson Pollock to explain the importance of each single drip. And it's difficult to believe the original writers were that scrupulous about their word choices, much less their designations of times and places.

Such precision will not engage the attention of this book, which is intended for the ordinary Christian trying to find a more personal insight into the mind of Christ expressed in these stories. For a more scholarly but still approachable treatment, see John R. Donahue, SJ, *The Gospel in Parables,* or Joachim Jeremias, *The Parables of Jesus.* Their finely tuned ears for word choices, customs, and stylistic quirks give a more reliable basis to judge whether this is the *ipsissima verba* (the very words) of Jesus or more likely a justifiable application of Jesus's mind to specific problems in the later communities of which he had no direct experience.

Nonetheless, here are a few pitfalls to avoid even in this book's treatments.

Intended to Confuse?

*W*hen the disciples asked Jesus why he spoke in parables instead of flat out like other teachers, he told them:

The reason I speak to them in parables is that "seeing they do not perceive, and hearing they do

not listen, nor do they understand." With them indeed is fulfilled the prophecy of Isaiah that says:
"You will indeed listen, but never un-
derstand,
and you will indeed look, but never
perceive." (Mt 13:13–14)

That passage could be misinterpreted to say that God somehow clouds the minds of unworthy people *purposely*, which would be sadistic, to say the least, and in no way compatible with the father of the prodigal son. One explanation might be obvious: If Jesus came out forthrightly and said "I am equal to God," he would not have lasted for three years.

More likely Jesus was saying that those capable of understanding would have to have hearts, minds, and souls that could see *beyond* strictly rational, step-by-step argumentation. Discovering his true meaning requires *more* than the thinking skills so prized by scientists, philosophers, and most educators. It takes a larger perspective even than the universe! Jesus, the evangelists, and their audiences *presumed* a dimension to reality that is by its very nature inaccessible to empirical scrutiny. Calculation and scholarship are essential, but they can take a person only so far. While faith is not a foolhardy "leap in the dark" based on no evidence, it also is not the kind of conclusion we can reach with calculus.

Let's put it more concretely. If Richard Dawkins, the brilliant atheist microbiologist, had been standing next to Mary Magdalene at the tomb of Jesus, would he have seen what she saw?

The Gospels are unanimous in testifying that those who had been closest to Jesus for three years and ingested (to a point) all his "doctrines" still found his physical return incomprehensible at first. It took *more* than logic, more even than the testimony of their senses (just as it does to accept the internal atomic mobility of everything our senses tell us is solid).

Hamlet said, "There are more things in Heaven and Earth, Horatio, than are dreamt of in your philosophy." Or your theology. Or even your physics. Could Plato have absorbed Darwin's endless growth? Could Galileo have accepted Einstein's curved space? The first sentence of Carl Sagan's *Cosmos* states categorically: "The cosmos is all there is, and all there ever was, and all there ever will be." At the core of the question of the meaning of religious faith is a further requirement of humility: How large are you personally willing to allow reality to be?

Reading scripture with the eyes of faith does *not* mean an intelligent reader must wall off everything he or she knows about science, psychology, cosmology, evolution, and so on in the left brain lobe, and all he or she knows of spirituality, salvation history, and God inaccessibly quarantined in the right lobe. But it does mean that believing will be more complex for the person who accepts *both at the same time*.

Physics—the hardest of the "hard sciences"—does that all the time! The electron is *both* a solid pellet *and* an ethereal wave at the same time. *Depending on how you look at it,* the chair you're sitting on is solid enough to hold you up, and yet it's swarming with particles, and most of it is empty space. Can you believe both?

The same humility might be invoked in regard to miracles. We have become used to accepting the impossibilities of inert matter starting to grow; vegetative matter beginning to uproot itself, move around, feel; and animal matter beginning to ask why. We simply take those miraculous transformations as givens. We forget that simply admitting those entities—rocks, rutabagas, and rats—simply don't have the potential within themselves to lift themselves to those higher levels. Even accepting a Creator at all forces one to accept that that Creator can do anything he damn well sets his mind to.

Beware Allegories

*B*ooks like *Pilgrim's Progress* make a point that every single character and place has a specific significance: Christian, Evangelist, Obstinate, Talkative, Feebleminded; Celestial City, Vanity Fair, River of Death. But with the parables, the temptation is to find U-2 flights where none was intended by Jesus or the evangelist. Even though Matthew (13:24–30) explains Jesus's story of the sower further (Jesus is the sower, the field is the world, the enemy is the devil, the reapers are angels), the other parables are more down to earth and less embroidered. And most scholars today claim Matthew probably went further than Jesus intended. That does not imply that Matthew's explanation is false, any more than a physicist's attempt to explain atoms falsifies the truth of it.

St. Augustine treated the Parable of the Good Samaritan that way: Jerusalem is heaven; Jericho is the moon, which means our mortality; the thieves are demons who strip the victim of immortality; the priest and Levite are the Old Testament; the innkeeper is the apostle Paul. Too much. It's just a story about kindness, not *Pilgrim's Progress*.

It would be unjustified to spin out the Parable of the Sower so that the hard ground is the flint hearts of Wall Street bankers, the shallow ground are hearts trivialized by media, and thorns are the encroachments of godless communism. As Freud is often attributed as saying, "Sometimes a cigar is just a cigar."

The Shock of Christianity

$\mathcal{M}$ost interested Christian readers have seen so many crucifixes that the best-intentioned readers find it hard to experience how jarring reports of the crucifixion must have been to its original listeners. Few of us are still aware that the symbol that captures the essence of Christianity is a statue of a corpse—a man utterly drained for others—who died to show he was human and rose to show he was God. The aware Christian looks at that symbol and says: "There is the most perfectly fulfilled human who ever lived, caught at the moment of his greatest triumph. I want to be like him." Contrary to our sensitivities even today, Christ asked his followers to forgive even their murderers, as he did. The two most basic elements of his life and lessons were healing and resurrection, forgiveness and starting over. Those unsettling lessons lie underneath any attempts to make Christianity a feel-good religion and ought to undercut any attempts to water it down.

In stark contrast to the contests by which we determine value—salaries, athletics, awards, tabloid attention—the objects of Jesus's concern were those whom Robert Farrar Capon singles out as "the last, the lost, the least, the little." And Jesus is "the Loser of God." Contrary to my early acquaintance with the Creator, the God of Jesus is no longer God Way Up There. In the Gospels the Divine Word—the Will of God—has "*become* flesh," shared our fatigue, rejection, doubt, temptations to despair. As St. Irenaeus writes, "I consider nothing human foreign to me."

The cross belies those poor souls who feel the burden of the world on their shoulders. It embodies the Christian truth that God has stepped in to take that on himself. Now we have to be humble enough to trust that he has reasons, that our sins are forgiven whenever we want them to be, that death is not the last word. It is impossible for us to earn what we already have.

Christianity was as seismic a break in human progress as the shift from inanimate matter into vegetative growth, and the change upward to sensitive animal life, and then the upward leap to rational cognition and self-consciousness. Humanity is now invited to enter into the aliveness of God—in Jesus Christ.

For many of us all such insights have become "desensitized" by textbooks and tests, calcified into doctrines instead of bold assertions of life. Jesus made that difference in understanding inescapable by comparing the kingdom to finding a treasure in a field. How many Christians have gone wild with delight at being Christian? At shedding fears of sin and death? Comprehending what Jesus did for us *should* have the effect that a full reprieve would have on a condemned convict! "There is no fear in love, but perfect love casts out fear; for fear has to do with punishment" (1 Jn 4:18).

Therefore, any valid extension of a parable's meaning should apply to the broadest audience, and with the most generous interpretation—since the whole life of Jesus, from his incarnation, through his life, passion, death, and resurrection was a continuous act of generosity.

Faith

*D*espite what "somebody" along the way has taught students I later end up teaching, faith is definitely *not* a blind leap in the dark. Such a leap is sheer idiocy. A girl tells her roommate, "My brother is really cute, smart, and ambitious," and her roommate says, "Great! I'll marry him!" A guy comes to your door and offers an acre of beach-front property in Florida for two thousand dollars, and you write the person a check. A phone call announces that you've won the lottery in Jamaica. All you need to do is wire cash for the taxes and the millions will be released to you. You immediately withdraw the money and send it. Some might say that anybody that gullible deserves the disenchanting results.

Genuine faith is a *calculated risk*. Whether belief in God or commitment to a marriage or agreement to build a house, trust is not a commitment only after one has undeniable evidence that compels assent nor is it a mindless leap on no evidence at all. But our modern expectations lean far more heavily toward the calculation than toward the risk. We want *security*. But in human commitments, certitude is simply impossible. The best "certainty" we can achieve is what Thomists call *moral certitude,* that is, "a high degree of probability," or, as the courts require, "beyond any *reasonable* doubt."

In understanding what was in Jesus's mind when he said, "Oh, you of little faith" or "Your faith has saved you," we have to realize the difference in understanding faith/belief/trust for a Jew and for a Greek.

The Greek mindset has had a much heavier influence on our present-day understanding. We want not only assurances and insurance, but "double-your-money-back" if we feel unsatisfied. Enough small print to double the length of a contract, covering every conceivable glitch. A cataract operation takes more time signing waivers than with the surgeon.

Contrarily, in the Eastern mindset (most of the non-European world) knowledge and trust were primarily established not by scrupulous intellectual examination and logic but by a person's trustworthiness established over time and experiences. The Hebrew word for "know," in fact, is rooted in the word for sexual intercourse, as in Old Testament passages like "And he knew his wife." Trustworthiness—the basis for faith-commitment—is based on proven loyalty, reliability.

Nonetheless, modern readers conditioned not only to skepticism but to capitalism want more evidence than used to uphold simple "peasant faith." That's why we need not only the gospel stories through which Jesus reveals *himself* as trustworthy but also scripture courses, apologetics courses, and doctrinal courses to explain the explanations.

The validity of the Gospels is not a house of cards. If we distrust one or two verses, the whole edifice doesn't come crumbling down. If we can accept that the limitless God became an up-country carpenter, died, and rose, all those petty "itches" fall back into perspective.

In the end of all the explanations and theologizing, this story of the lone mountain climber rings true. He's just yards from the summit when he suddenly slips through the rubble, right over the edge of the cliff, and hangs on to a tough bush anchored in the rock. "Help!" he hollers. "Is there anybody up there?" Panicky and sweating, he hears a great booming voice: "This is God. Let go. I'll catch you!" The climber thinks a moment. Then he hollers, "Is there anybody *else* up there?"

Nope.

Part I

Story Parables

With Jesus, however, the device of parabolic utterance is used not to explain things to people's satisfaction but to call attention to the unsatisfactoriness of all their previous explanations and understandings.

—Robert Farrar Capon

*J*esus's first word was always "peace." But he didn't mean *peace* in the way many of us think of it: being unbothered, escaping to some Gauguin island in the South Seas, avoiding conflict, or even attention. His idea of peace is much more dynamic and vital than that—the peace of the tightrope walker, nurses in terminal wards, those who defuse bombs.

The reason for the reductionism that subdues Jesus into *only* the Good Shepherd, meek and mild, is that well-meaning teachers try to make Jesus a model to control the Beast in us, especially in unruly boys. They expunge the rowdy Jesus the Temple hierarchy found too dangerous to tolerate and left only the Jesus who was sinless yet startlingly empathetic to weakness, the bearded-lady Jesus of the saccharine holy pictures, the Jesus who rejected the sword Peter tried to defend him with at his arrest. All true. But only half-truth.

Those who hanged Christ on a cross didn't execute him because he was just a nice, moral teacher who wanted us to be unbothersome. You don't crucify an irrelevance. They hanged him because he was a menace to their complacency, because—like Gandhi and Martin Luther King, Jr., who met the same fate—he came to empower the powerless. They killed him because he knew who God called him to be and refused to shut up about it.

When the lion lies down with the lamb, we naturally expect the lion to become lamblike. In too many classes and homilies about Jesus, the Lamb of God devours the Lion of Judah, rather than vice versa. But clearly, the way Jesus acted, the lion lies down with the lamb but *retains* its leonine ferocity. It becomes disciplined but not domesticated into a big, smiling pussycat. Jesus didn't turn the other cheek to the hypocritical Pharisees or to Peter when he tried to block him from Jerusalem or to the Temple moneychangers. At those moments his righteous rage would have been sin to suppress.

There are times when a Christian *can't* be silent, when we have to make a disturbance—no matter how unpleasant for those around us and, indeed, for ourselves. "I have come to cast fire on the earth—I come not for peace but for division" (see Lk 12:49-51).

If that gospel passage doesn't unnerve us, we've never really heard the real gospel.

1.

The Kindly Outcast

LUKE 10:29–37

*O*nce upon a time, not that long ago, there was a Jerusalem merchant named Mordecai. Considering the early hour, Mordecai knew he was God's own fool for setting off down the road to Jericho alone. Anyone in possession of his wits would have waited for the midmorning caravan. But he had an impatient client in Jericho at midafternoon, so off he went.

The high road from the city to Jericho was only eighteen miles, steeply downhill all the way. But it would take eight hours, through rock-walled passes. About five miles out, he approached the Adumin Rocks, the Bloody Pass. Some said the name came from its red rock walls. Others claimed it was from the blood bandits had shed there.

Suddenly, they were there. A half dozen men sprang from the rocks on either side of the road, faces muffled in the tails of their turbans. They flung themselves on him. Two tore the reins of his pack mule from his fist and dragged her away. The others manhandled him off his mount and hauled him to the edge over the deep bushy ditch, cutting his purse from his belt. They ripped off his tunic and shirt, pummeling his face and body. Blood burst from his broken nose, and they hurled him, near naked, banging down the rocks into the brush.

They were gone as quickly as they had come.

Two hours later the caravan came rumbling down the steep dirt road, camels chewing abstractedly on their cuds, chains rattling, drovers cursing them along with their heels. Pilgrims from the north were returning home, avoiding the hostile roads in Samaria for the road east of the Jordan. Pack mules hunched under loads of trade goods—earthen pots, clanking cleavers, and sheep bells. Three or four hired muscle sat atop skittish horses, eyes peeled for any suspicious movements among the rock formations and down among the weed-choked ditches. Otherwise, as indifferent as the camels.

Along the outside edge of the road, away from the rock face, a Temple priest caught sight of what seemed to be a body down below among the rocks. He nudged his companion, a Levite professor of the Law, who looked and saw the same figure. But he pinched his brows and shrugged, and the two continued on. They had the Lord's business on their minds.

After the cavalcade rumbled by, and its dust just began to settle, came the dregs—pickpockets and mountebanks with jars of panaceas, street people hoping for the fatter purses of the spa visitors in Jericho, softer than tight-fisted city folks. Street walkers sought newer horizons. Riding a hundred yards or so behind them all, leading his pack donkey laden with goods he had bartered his small sheep herd for at Temple prices, came a peddler. A Samaritan traveling home, close enough for the protection of the caravan but not close enough to hear the contempt even the camp-following rejects had for half-breeds. He whistled as he went, to keep up his spirits.

As he peered downward from atop his bumpy mule, he spied a flash of unexpected white and crimson in the brambles below. He slipped off his mount, held back his pack mule, and peered over the edge. It was a man's back, bare and covered in bloody gashes.

He hauled the mule's reins over her head and sidled down the rockfall through the bushes. He was a hill man, but he had no skills for falling. Gradually, he sidled down to the body, grip by grip, half-conscious of his foolhardiness. If it was a man, what in heaven's name was he going to do with him? And he was probably already dead by the look of him.

And it was a man, stripped naked and bloodied all over, but breathing. His eyes were purplish black. The peddler hooked his hands into the man's armpits and, grunting upward, step by step, feeling the next niche above, he lugged the battered fellow up the cliffside. Three times he had to stop to get his breath, feeling his arms and legs tremble with the strain.

Finally, he lifted the man up onto the road and fell in a heap, the heavy weight across his knees.

He eased the body off and went to his pack animal, untying one of the wineskins and grabbing the rag he used to wipe down the mules. He stumbled over to the beaten man and slowly washed his body with wine, grateful the man was unconscious.

When he finished, he led his donkey over and grunting with effort pulled the body up into his arms again, and with a heave got the man belly down over the donkey's back. He took the reins of both the mule and the donkey and began to climb back up the road, back toward the city.

It was another five miles up the steep slope to the city, but there were inns on the outskirts. He could leave him at one for the rest of the day and overnight.

The poor wretch would be safe now. If he was late getting to Jericho, so be it.

Thoughts to Ponder

∽ Remember the *framework*. The story was occasioned by a law expert trying to make Jesus narrow the focus of "needy neighbor." Jesus does a typical turnabout and asks who *acted* like a neighbor. Samaritans were pariahs to upright Jews. They held only the first five books of the scripture, refused to worship in the Temple, and so were heretics. In the Assyrian invasion they had intermarried and were thus half-breeds. The mutual hatred was as old—and ill considered—as the Hatfields and the McCoys, and as deadly as the long and cruel racial animosity in nearly every culture, including our own.

It does give the thoughtful Christian pause, however. Too easy to disdain the complacent priest and Levite, and yet few but the certified saints are without their unreasoned biases. Illegal immigrants, overweight girls, unathletic boys, rap "artists," homosexuals.

∽ The *priest and Levite* did nothing "wrong." No law obligated them to risk their safety for a stranger. And they could assure themselves that it only *seemed* to be a body. And human. It might not even be a Jew. And they did have important religious business.

The episode shows clearly the difference between justice and Jesus. What differentiates the doctrines of Christ from legalism is basic human decency. In Jesus's Parable of the Last Judgment (Mt 25), there is only one question to determine readiness for heaven. Not "How often did you pray or stray? Yield to weakness?" but

"I was hungry, thirsty, naked. . . . What did you do?" In effect, "Were you kind?"

🌿 *False humility.* The best way to short circuit a crusade to set souls on fire is a concerted campaign to get all the candidates to bow their heads and groan, "Oh, I'm nobody!" But that's what kind folks have whispered to us since we were in diapers: "Don't be proud! Don't become *vain*!" What could be more unchristian? Look what the One calling managed to get out of Abraham and Sarah, who were in their nineties and barren as a pair of bricks. And Moses, who stammers for about fifty lines, trying to weasel out of the invitation. And poor Jeremiah trying to beg off because "I'm only a boy." All heroes were unlikely prospects: Our Lady, St. Peter, Joan of Arc, Francis of Assisi, Martin Luther, John XXIII, Nelson Mandela, Mother Teresa—all faceless nobodies who finally said, "I'm mad as hell, and I'm not gonna take it any more!" And all those little nobodies upended the world. Jumped up and down and made the parade take a new tack.

🌿 *Overkill.* In our culture we're bombarded every day by victims in ditches—from TV, pages of glossy magazines, the news. And there are just so many of them—starving kids with flies drinking their tears, babies devoured alive by AIDS, kids caught in wars almost everyone on earth hates. We seem to have only two choices. One extreme is to erect barriers to the stimuli, impenetrable unless they're grossly intrusive, like sirens. We become inured to them, like graffiti and litter. Like the priest and the Levite, we may say, "Oh, God, another one. But I'm only a single person. What can I do?" And get on with our lives.

At the other extreme (where most of us are) are those afflicted by the so-called liberal guilt complex. Somehow, we're responsible for everything. Which is, in a very true way, well-meaning blasphemy. Only God has exclusive claim to that. True, there's something wrong with our heart if, like the priest and Levite, we can turn the page or click the channel without at least mumbling, "Oh, my God." But no matter how good-hearted or well-heeled we are, we can't help them all. Not even a major part of them. Remember: There were hundreds of lepers in Palestine that Jesus didn't and couldn't cure. But each of us can do something for somebody.

∾ *Prudent kindness.* It's probably imprudent to stop to help a car broken down on the highway. It could be a ploy, even though most times it's not. But it's only a minor inconvenience to note the landmarks and stop at the next roadside phone to call 911. Even easier with a cell phone. The same probably holds true for a drunk in a doorway. We help the ones you can, just as Jesus did. Second, when a panhandler sticks out his paw, we give him what we can—even if he's the third one that day. No matter what his reason, we have it on the highest authority that he's Jesus in disguise. And we need to give it with a smile, not just to get him out of our face. Don't ponder how he'll spend it. When we give a gift certificate, we don't say, "Now be sure to spend that on something I'd approve of." Third, we can pick out a worthwhile charity and send it the cost of a meal once a month. Check out the worthy ones. I logged on to the Better Business Bureau website and out it popped: all the major charities with a pie graph of how much of their income actually goes to the needy and not management or advertising. The

Osmond Foundation for Kids disperses 90 percent, Catholic Relief Services 82 percent, Project Hope 92 percent, the Multiple Sclerosis Society only 41 percent. It's all right there on the Internet. Fourth, we can go through our closets and bureaus and pull out anything we haven't worn in a year. We obviously don't need it, and it might save someone's life—or at least provide the lift of having a new shirt.

We can't save them all. Neither could Jesus. But we, by God, can surely save some.

꒰ *Honest love.* This isn't a feeling. Love's an act of will, a commitment that takes over when feelings fail, when the beloved is no longer even likable. Love's very undramatic: taking out the garbage love, getting up to change the baby love, letting go of the grudge love. Animals can feel affection, even to the point of giving up their lives for their own babies. But we can give up our lives—often without dying—for people we don't even like. Ask any parent. Or teacher.

There are a lot of victims by the side of our road. We pass by them every day. We know, at least vaguely, who they are. We can't help all of them. There are too many, and some might even resent our offer of help. But why not pick just one? One we suspect *wouldn't* repel an offer of kindness? It is, after all, the only basis on which we can claim the word *Christian.*

2.

The Spendthrift's Father
LUKE 15:11–24

*O*nce upon a time, a widower named Baruch owned a small, successful plantation, a chain of tenant farms raising grain and cattle. Baruch tended the fields around his home with the help of quite a few servants and his two sons. The other properties he rented to tenant families for a fair share of their harvests.

Caleb, the elder son, was twenty and engaged to be married. A fine lad: guileless, dutiful, dependable, and humorless as bedrock. His brother, Asher, was days before his eighteenth birthday, just the opposite of his brother—quicksilver, bubbling with life, far too free with the servants, even with the girls. But his spirit was contagious, and it took a foul disposition and a deal of effort to dislike him or rope him in. Each boy was precious to his father in his own way.

One day young Asher came to Baruch and said, abruptly, "Father, I'm eighteen. There's no real future for me here. I'll never be a farmer. Or a landlord. And you know it would kill me to take orders from Caleb. Give me my share of the inheritance now. Caleb will get two-thirds, and I'll get my one-third. I'm really not depriving him. This way, I could go to the city. Learn a trade. Or apprentice myself to an artist. Please, father."

Baruch sat stunned, hardly able to get his breath. Was this the son he loved? As good as wishing him dead? He tried to speak. "But, Asher . . . "

"I know it's not usual. But it's been done."

"Asher, even if I make my will for you to inherit, you can't sell those properties until I'm dead. Once I write the will, even I can't sell them."

"Of course, father. But I could use them as surety for a loan."

"But you're only eighteen."

"And how will I learn how to handle money without handling money? By the time I inherit, I'll still be like a child in my head."

Knowing full well what a fool he was being, Baruch drew up the papers assigning one-third of all he had worked a lifetime for to his younger son. Perhaps the boy was right. The properties would come to him anyway, sooner or later. He was bright, and he would never yield to farm life. He just might learn a trade— and learn manhood at the same time. Baruch had to admit, even with work on the farm, the boy had been spoiled. He needed toughening up.

So, Asher set out on one of the mules for the seaport of Caesarea. Secure in his saddlebag were his inheritance papers and a letter of credit from his father's banker sufficient for passage to some nearby city where emigrant Jews had gathered in large numbers. It was only a day's travel to the coast, but along the tedious way he could often hardly believe the wonders of the real world. After one night in the cheapest inn on the docks, he bought passage for himself and the mule on a merchant ship up the Phoenician coast seventy miles to Antioch in Syria. He could have gone by land in a day or two, but the ship was safer and he was eager to confront his destiny.

It was the first time in his life he'd had money of his own, to spend as he pleased.

Antioch was one of the largest cities on earth, crossroads of the empire, and when he landed he was speechless with awe at the life, the noise, the colors. Streets were clogged with clamorous, knockabout traffic, bands of jugglers and snake dancers, slave girls bedecked for the market, cohorts on the march, merchants from Baghdad and Damascus with silks, spices, and perfumes, beefy gladiators, men with caged beasts for the circus. Beyond his wildest dreams.

He quickly engaged a room in what he was told was a Jewish enclave, probably too expensive but all right until he could get settled. Right away he found a banker named Nesher, pleased to honor his father's letter of credit. However, it took Asher a day to forge the courage to approach another Jewish banker named Bachel with his great lie. His father had recently died, Asher claimed, and he would like to exchange the deeds to his father's tenant farms for cash. He was naive enough not to grasp that he was also selling all future revenues. He knew the man was a professional vulture and what he received was far less than the deeds could be sold for to some banker back home, but it was more cash than Asher had ever thought possible. For a trivial fee Bachel was willing to hold most of the cash ready for withdrawal whenever the lad requested it.

There was meat every day, even ostrich or flamingo, and wine far better than vinegar. And friends. Many young men, once they saw how comfortable and innocent he was, found him charming, mingling and gossiping with him in the baths and at the arena and taverns. In Antioch fashion was the only law, pleasure the only pursuit. It was a city of consumers, aristocrats, and retired newly rich. Here every niche of life was up to date, amusing, elegant, wicked.

Of course, it couldn't last. The inheritance wasn't a prince's ransom to begin with. But it had seemed that way. Asher tried his best to keep an eye on what he had left, but Bechel seemed to do it far better. The boy pleaded for a loan but had nothing to secure it with. He roamed the streets looking for work, and finally he was reduced to begging, just to eat. He resisted offers to degrade himself, but finally he became so desperate he took a job tending pigs, the most loathsome animals on earth, ready to silence his groaning belly with the pulp of the carob pods he fed them.

Finally, after months of degradation, he came to his senses. Envying swine. "The worst looking beggar at my father's gate isn't this desperate. Enough. I'll go home. My father is a good man. He'll let me come back. If not from love, from charity. Yes. He will."

So he set off on the long journey south, homeward, begging his food, sleeping in ditches. Along the way he rolled his apology over and over in his head: "Father, I've sinned against God and against you. I don't deserve to be your son. But could you hire me? I'll work hard to make it up to you. Not just the money. . . . Father, I've sinned against . . . "

Meanwhile, back home, as every evening before the evening meal, Baruch was out on the hill above his house, peering down his road to the highway, hoping. For so many nights, nothing.

But tonight he saw a speck far off, a late traveler. He waited an interminable time till the figure came into focus. It was a ragged young man. Stumbling. Alone.

Asher.

Baruch began to move slowly down the hill. Then suddenly he was sure. It ill befitted the master to run, but he *ran*! His heart galloped faster than his feet. My *son*!

The weary boy looked up the path to the house and saw his father. Running. He stopped and stood in wonder.

Baruch collided with the young man and clutched him to his chest and kissed him.

"Father," Asher mumbled into his father's shoulder.

"Hush," his father said. "Hush! My *son*!"

"Father, I've sinned against God and against you. I . . . "

"Enough," the old man said, dragging him in his arms up toward the house. "Enoch," he shouted for his steward. "Quick! Bring water! And fresh clothes! And shoes!"

His foreman appeared on the porch, bewildered.

"Bring his family ring. And sandals. He can't go round like a slave. And tell the cook! The calf for the feast! We'll have it tonight. Send men to invite the tenants. And their families!"

"Master," Enoch said, still mystified.

"Now, man! Now! My son who was dead is alive again! *Alive*!"

Thoughts to Ponder

∾ *God, the Father*. This father sees his child from afar, implying he's been out there every evening, waiting, praying, hoping. And the father runs to the boy, not the other way around, despite the fact it was beneath the dignity of any Hebrew father or landowner to run for any reason. And he throws his arms around the kid and kisses him, *before* the boy has gotten out more than a single word of his memorized apology! There's no demand, like, "I want to know how you wasted every single shekel of my money before you get back into my house!" There's no self-serving, vindictive demand that the foolish boy grovel. "My son who was dead is alive again!" Life is more important than money. And this father demands no penance. Instead, he gives the sinner a party! That is the God that Jesus reveals.

The parable is usually called the Parable of the Prodigal Son because the boy is so improvident with money he did nothing to merit. But the father is the one who is, in a much deeper sense, rash, incautious, foolhardy. The younger boy isn't just bold but brazenly offensive, insolent, ungrateful. And his father simply goes along with it. Gives the boy his freedom. Not just that, but gifts aplenty, enough to last a lifetime with careful management.

Our Father does the same. Gives us life when nothing we could do would deserve his gift. Sheer incomprehensible love. And so many gifts we take for granted—miraculous bodies, people who love us, work to take pride in. Even more, though, in giving us freedom, God curtailed his own unlimited freedom. He gave this one species the ability to say no to him.

This parable is simply one more retelling of Adam and Eve. Neither story ever historically happened, but both are true.

～ *Freedom.* Like forgiveness, freedom is one of the hardest gifts to give our children. Even in simple things: leaving them at the preschool door; giving them the keys to the car and saying, "OK, take it out alone"; the first date; not reading their emails. Then the wedding, wanting to intrude with advice, allowing them to learn from their own mistakes. It takes real love.

∽ *True love*. Affection is spontaneous, and genuine love may often be spontaneous as well, but a great many times we give real love with our teeth clenched. It may be freely given, but it's rarely easy. Bona fide love isn't in the love songs: "I can't live without you. . . . That old black magic has me in its spell. . . . Love can make you waste in sorrow and die." Those are being-in-love songs, thump-thump "romance." Very dramatic—and to the objective viewer, self-dramatizing. *"Romeo and Juliet, West Side Story,* soap operatic, love drunk.

Nothing wrong with that. In fact, absolutely marvelous. Who would stand up in front of a couple hundred people and vow responsibility for another human being till one dies—without being pixilated on love potion? Romance is a marvelous place to visit. But you can't really live there too long. Prince Charming occasionally shape-shifts into a werewolf; Cinderella at times betrays qualities formerly associated with her venomous stepsisters.

Real love, genuine love, is most often very undramatic, even "domesticated," unlike the ferocity of being-in-love. Real love is stirring the pasta love, "No, go back to sleep; I'll get up and change her" love; cutting down on the drinking love. Real love says, "I want you to be happy, even if you're a bit of a hemorrhoid right now. I'd rather be unhappy with you than happy with someone else. I love you even if, at the moment, I'm having real difficulty liking you."

∽ Think of *Simon Peter*, the first pope. It defies imagining to conceive of John XXIII or John Paul II or Pope Francis in blatant apostasy, publicly denying Jesus, bolstered with fierce curses. To a couple of *waitresses*! Yet that's precisely what the first pope did. And Jesus still chose him over the wily Judas, the ethereal John, and the worldly wise Matthew. It defies reason.

After the resurrection we have no evidence that Jesus taxed Peter for his cowardice, not even obliquely, as we just might be tempted to do. Instead, in that lovely scene on Lake Tiberias, when big-hearted Peter pulls *on* clothes to jump into the surf to go to Jesus, the Lord just says, "Come, have breakfast." Then as they lounge companionably around the fire, Jesus asks, "Simon, son of John, do you truly love me?"

Try to imagine the pulsing conflict in Peter's guts between shame and love, the yearning for the words to compensate. All he can say, helplessly, is, "Lord, you know all things; you know I love you." Three times, Jesus asks, and three times Peter answers—the same number of times he had betrayed his friend. And with that trivial recompense—for Peter's neediness!—Jesus reinstated him as the first of them. "Feed my lambs. Feed my sheep." Into the hands of this man who had proven himself so imperfect, he returned the keys of the kingdom of God.

3.

The Dutiful Son

LUKE 15: 25–32

Toward dinner time, Baruch's older son, Caleb, led his crew of hired men toward the main house from the wheat fields. A backbreaking day, stoop work, hacking at the relentless weeds. They were all begrimed and sweaty, heading to the trough.

Caleb felt good. This crop was as good as it gets.

But as they came to the road up to the house, they heard music—flutes and drums and clapping hands, loud laughter from many people. And the smell of cooking meat.

As they climbed the hill, the sounds and smells grew more intense. Caleb saw a kitchen boy trotting from the cookhouse to the front steps.

"You, boy!" Caleb called.

The boy hesitated between delivering his dish and the new master.

"What's going on?" Caleb demanded.

"Your brother, Asher, Master Caleb!" The boy huffed. "He's back. Safe and sound! Your father's thrown a big party! Killed the calf we were saving for the feast."

Caleb's heart tensed. "Is he . . . is my brother well?"

"Oh, no, Master Caleb. You should have seen him. We had to scrub him raw! He's had a terrible time. He lost . . . he lost everything."

Everything. Gambling? Women? Wild schemes? The no-good . . .

Caleb stood rooted to the hard ground. He gestured to his men. "Go in. Go in."

"Aren't you coming?" one asked.

"I'll die first," Caleb muttered.

He stood with his arms folded, resolute as a fence post.

Only a few moments later, Baruch appeared on the porch. "Caleb?"

The young man did not look up. His father came slowly down to him and put his hand on his shoulder. "What's the matter? Asher is home!"

"Oh, is he?"

"Come in, Caleb. Your brother's alive. Bruised and battered, but he's alive!"

Caleb drew in a deep breath. "I'm told he lost it all. All our money."

Baruch nodded sadly. "A terrible price to pay to begin to become wise."

"A terrible price? To whores and crooks and gamblers?"

"But he's still our Asher, Caleb."

"Our Asher? After he treated you like you were dead? I suppose he sold the deeds, too, yes? And you let him walk back in here like he missed a day of shul? Broke a jug?"

"But your brother's more important than the money, son."

"And more important than loyalty. And respect."

Baruch didn't know how to touch his son's heart.

Caleb gave a sour smile. "What does *Caleb* have to do to get a party? Lose the rest of your money and land? I could probably learn how to do that."

"Caleb . . . "

"I've slaved for you ever since I was a kid. I never disobeyed, never gave you less than my best. And you never gave me even a ropy goat for a party with my friends. But this . . . this son of yours comes home . . . after he's thrown all you've worked for to the winds . . . gambling, whoring . . . and you want to celebrate because he's back for *more*? It makes no sense! It's disgusting!"

"My son," Baruch squeezed the young man's shoulder, "you've always been my son. I'm sorry if I took you for granted. And you now have all that was mine. Please. Come. Your brother is come back from the *dead*!"

But Caleb stood immovable. Baruch hesitated, then turned and walked back up the steps.

And the damnable music kept on and on.

Thoughts to Ponder

∽ *Second chances*. This section of Luke's Gospel includes the parallel Parable of the Lost Sheep and the Parable of the Lost Coin, both attesting to God's refusal to give up on us, no matter what. And they are framed by the occasion Luke chose to focus his guess about the *initial* audience.

Now all the tax collectors and sinners were coming near to listen to him. And the Pharisees and the scribes were grumbling and saying, "This fellow welcomes sinners and eats with them" (Lk 15:1–2).

So it seems that Luke believed Jesus wanted to contrast his way of manifesting God and the way of the scribes and Pharisees. Unlike the sinners Jesus so uncritically consorted with, the Temple servants were the "elder brother." But it would be wrong to over-read the conclusions, misled by the caricatures of grotesquely wicked Pharisees in biblical films. The gospel writers, especially Matthew, as we saw earlier, are harsher on the Pharisees than the historical record suggests they deserved. The reason was that, as he wrote, his own people were being ostracized, disowned, even physically punished for apostatizing from Judaism to this new sect.

In this story, the elder brother could well have been the officials of Judaism. But we cannot justify *by the story* any suggestion that Jesus *rejects* them, as if the generous father (God) revoked his elder son's inheritance as punishment for his lack of forgiveness. He doesn't do that here. He still loves his older son. He merely cajoles him, asks him to open his heart.

For the most part the historical Pharisees were genuinely good people—diligent, reliable, respectable, trying to serve God in the best way they knew how. To judge them otherwise would be to adopt the same unyielding pharisaic judgmentalism portrayed in the movies.

∿ Led, perhaps, by that *oversimplification*, some have too readily called the elder brother self-righteous, self-centered, just plain mean-spirited. But he had done his *best*. And he was *hurt*. He had never received such evidence of his father's love. Why? Because he never seemed to *need* it. (Till I proof read this chapter the fifth time, it had never occurred to me that—as the original story stands—nobody seemed to have thought to send word out to the fields about the party.)

But that raises another interesting question: What was the real *motive* for the elder brother's sulk? Was he angry because his brother had the prize calf killed for him and wanted one himself, or is it that he resented his wayward *brother* having it? Was he angry at his brother or at his father? ("*you* never . . . this son of *yours . . . you* killed . . . ")

St. John Chrysostom preached, "Almost any decent person can weep with those who weep, but very few of us can rejoice with those who rejoice."

      ∽ *Dutifulness*. Rather than a nasty indictment of the elder son, this half of the parable Jesus told rests not on judgment but on the hope the older brother might come to respect himself more, to see his true value to his father, not a servant but his son. W. H. Auden wrote an ironic poem called "To an Unknown Citizen," quietly lamenting those good, dutiful folks who do what they are told and miss everything God meant humans to be:

> He was found by the Bureau of Statis-
>   tics to be
> One against whom there was no official
>   complaint,
> And all the reports on his conduct
>   agree
> That, in the modern sense of an old-
>   fashioned word, he was a saint,
> For in everything he did he served the
>   Greater Community.
>   . . .

When there was peace, he was for peace:
    when there was war, he went.
He was married and added five chil-
    dren to the population,
Which our Eugenist says was the right
    number for a parent of his gen-
    eration.
And our teachers report that he never
    interfered with their education.
Was he free? Was he happy? The ques-
    tion is absurd:
Had anything been wrong, we should
    certainly have heard.

     Love need. Is there any one of us who does not feel under-appreciated? Is there something *wrong* with wanting to be thanked? If we live among those who claim to be loving Christians, what fault is there in wishing they practiced what they preach?

> Above all, maintain constant love for one another, for love covers a multitude of sins. Be hospitable to one another without complaining. Like good stewards of the manifold grace of God, serve one another with whatever gift each of you has received. Whoever speaks must do so as one speaking the very words of God. (1 Pt 4:8–11)

Love is hardly genuine when the impetus behind it is shrouding our other faults. It's more intimidating—and likely more consistent with Jesus's understanding—to accept that we are conduits of God's grace and that, no matter how unimportant we feel, we are capable of blocking the mercy of an omnipotent God.

4.

The Great Banquet
MATTHEW 22:1–14

*O*nce upon a time, back when people were not as honest as they are now, there was an ambitious tax collector named Aqubba. He had started his ascent to riches and power as the town tough, but worked his way shrewdly, steadily up the crooked ladder to become district tax commissioner. Aqubba was detested beyond words for collaborating with the abominable Roman invaders and skimming his hefty percentage off the crushing taxes of his neighbors.

Partly to save his son from the local ruffians, Aqubba had sent the boy to Rome for a proper education. Now the boy had returned and was about to be married, so his father planned a colossal banquet and sent formal invitations to all the landed gentry in the area to introduce his son and his intended to society, convinced that—if his fabulous wealth had yet to perfume his past—everyone would now fight for places at a meal destined for legend.

Aqubba's servants scoured the countryside for the finest meats, vegetables, fruits, cheeses, and wines. Cooks and chefs let their imaginations run wild and worked their helpers to exhaustion. A small army of servants set up tables with stools and divans for hundreds of guests and decorated the enormous hall as if for a visit from the emperor.

No one came.

Aqubba fumed. "Send men out there," he stormed at his steward, "and bring in every cripple they can find. Everybody blind, maimed, and misborn. Haul in every hag with her hand stuck out for alms. Bring in even the *fakes*! Bring the garbage pickers. I want this room filled with people eating and drinking, having *fun*!"

So they did. Gradually, the tables began to fill. Paralytics were brought in and laid with their pallets right on the dining couches like visiting nobles; old beggars primped in their threadbare tunics; blind folks sat erect on stools, too timid to move lest they knock over something costly. All of them were nervous. Afraid it was some trick to mock them.

But the great hall was still half empty.

Aqubba looked over the room and snapped, "Send them out again. Get the *real* riffraff this time. The doorway drunks, down-at-the heel whores, pickpockets, the sidewalk pawnbrokers and gamblers, round up all the families camped out there in the tombs.

So they did. Finally, when the room was filled and the music began, the party goers very slowly began to lose their fears of a hoax, to smile cautiously, to nod to their neighbors and share names. After a while, they began to laugh.

Aqubba smiled. It was better than he had hoped.

But his steward approached Aqubba and said, "Master, I need your advice. I realize these people are . . . are not the quality of persons the servants are used to . . . uh . . . serving. But there is one . . . uh, gentleman, who is making . . . well, rather a nuisance. Annoying the other guests. What would you like us to do with him?"

"Take me to him," Aqubba said.

When they got to the unwelcome guest, it took no wit to see he had already had a great deal more to drink than he needed. He was roaring insults at the people reclining near him, who all would have seemed beyond further insult.

"My friend," Aqubba said, laying his hand on the man's shoulder.

"And who," the man burbled, "are you, my fren'?"

"I am your host."

"Well, how nice for you."

"You're making my guests uncomfortable. We'd like you to be generous to them as we've been generous to you."

"Oh, like to Madame Lah-De-Da over there who shares herself with the army swine, and My Lord Crook down the line who lines up schoolboy thieves?"

"And you're thieving their enjoyment."

"But you invited me, now di'n't you?"

"And I now disinvite you." He nodded to the steward and the nearby waiters. "Take him out of here. He's upsetting my worthy guests. Throw him out with the swill."

So four stout young men lifted him up over their heads and carried him to the back door, with him protesting the unfair treatment all the way. "I was *invited*!" And they hurled him into the dark.

Thoughts to Ponder

◝ *The Unwelcome Guest.* Notice that I shifted the metaphor at the end of the story (which is only in Matthew, an addition not in Luke's version of the same story). Matthew says the reason the man at the end was singled out was his lack of proper clothing. Some try to avoid the issue by claiming there was a rack of proper garments at the door, though there is no evidence in the story for that. The point is that—for whatever reason—the intruder did *not* fit in.

But *none* of them fit in! None of them had the dubious qualities that recommended those who refused to come to the party of the *nouveau riche* host. But here, as one comes to expect from Jesus, everything about the physically disabled and the social misfits qualified them to be there. That's the whole point of the story. Nobody *deserved* to be there.

To insist on the literalism of the garment is a direct denial of what Jesus himself said in Matthew's treatment of the Sermon on the Mount: "And why do you worry about clothing? Consider the lilies of the field, how they grow; they neither toil nor spin, yet I tell you, even Solomon in all his glory was not clothed like one of these" (Mt 6:28–29).

Moreover, the punishment is much too severe for a mere "wardrobe malfunction."

Therefore, the rejection had nothing to do with surface issues—even, as I've reworked it, to annoying behavior. Something *inside* him was "off." His attitude.

"Many are called, but few are chosen." Grace is freely given, but it's useless unless it's accepted—and used. Baptism alone gives no one a claim. Even being poor or a sinner is no guarantee of belonging. The new life ignites only if we feel the need for it. Accepting the call means *conversion*, a complete turnabout, an inner change. The invitation was universal but not totally indiscriminate.

Years ago a former student asked me to preside at his wedding.

"Are you both practicing Catholics?"

"No, in fact she's Jewish, and we'll raise the children Jewish. Not for religious reasons but ethnic reasons."

"Do you practice at all, even a couple times a year?"

"No."

"Do you have any real relationship with God?"

"Well, no."

"Then why do you want a priest and a mass?"

"Well, I'm still a Catholic."

∾ *Grudging Christians* are contradictions. "Look, I showed up, didn't I?" But just showing up isn't enough. This is a gathering of subversives, an underground army dedicated to the overthrow of "the world." Every week we come together to bolster our courage and our resolve to undermine smugness with vulnerability, to counter greed with generosity, to face self-absorbed nastiness with forgiveness.

We're talking two different parties here: the kingdom party, where the halfhearted really have no place, and the world party, where the unselfish stand out like skunks at a garden tea. Perversely, our purpose is to be to the world's orgy what the grungy guest was to the banquet of the kingdom: eyesores making them uncomfortable with their self-absorbed hedonism, making them suspect by our joy that they might be missing something. We seem to enjoy the week as much as the weekends; we might be getting more fun out of living than they are.

∾ *Cradle Catholics* had it easy. We "bought" the shocking claims of the gospel before we could think critically, when we still believed in Santa Claus, had no difficulty believing snakes once spoke to nudists in a park, accepted that guts and spunk and wits could ultimately melt all the wicked witches. That's why Jesus said only those as gullible and prone to awe (and humility) as children could find his kingdom. I suspect that children may have a privileged viewpoint on what's really possible, an inroad to the truth we've surrendered for a colossal urbane shallowness.

"You want to know who's the first in the kingdom?" And he lifts up a child. That's the cost of entering the Body of Christ: to become a child. But that's impossible. Like telling Nicodemus he had to be born again. Yet I think Jesus really meant that: that we have to start over. That's the whole gospel.

How do we get our childhood back? Go for a walk in the woods alone with God, and be vulnerable, childlike—as God is childlike. God's never grown old, never become sophisticated, disenchanted, world weary. Learn to paint, sketch, putter with clay, garden—as God did with us in the beginning.

~ Just in case: This story cannot be read as equating Christianity with *merely being mannerly,* nonintrusive, biddable, polite. Jesus showed no deference to his clergy or to the well placed. He rousted businessmen licensed by the Temple in a most unrighteous way. He breached a whole series of time-honored traditions. He intended to be disruptive.

5.

The Feisty Widow
Luke 18:2–8

*O*nce upon a time, long ago, before there were investigative reporters, there was this really corrupt judge, a hawk-faced, flint-hearted scoundrel named Ayah. He'd been appointed by the Romans to adjudicate disputes between Jews and Romans. This old guy feared *no one*, not even God. Maybe the Roman occupation. But he had a quite healthy respect for silver and gold.

In the same town there was an aging widow named Emunah whose husband had left her with little more than her house and the land surrounding it, which was next to the compound of the Roman town garrison. The officer in charge had commandeered half of her property to build a bath house for his men, and he had promised fair compensation. She had no income, so she agreed. But when the payment came, it was only half the agreed price.

Day after day she showed up at the compound, but the officer treated her like a bad smell. Finally, she took the matter to Judge Ayah. For hours she waited while, one after another, rich men had their cases settled quickly, Ayah's judgment paid for before he had even heard the case. Emunah's petition was handled even more quickly, since each day the judge simply refused to consider it, not wanting to alienate the Roman officer.

The case was moot. She was a woman—poor, childless, friendless, and alone.

But Emunah resolved she would not be beaten. Each day, when Judge Ayah took his nap after the noon meal, she had the neighborhood children dance outside his windows, chanting, "Judge Ayah's soul is dead and cold. Comes from eating too much gold. Judge Ayah's soul . . . " Then she'd hush them a few moments with bits of honeycake till Ayah could fall asleep. Then she'd start them again, some improvising on reed whistles: "Judge Ayah's soul . . . " When the servants tried to shoo them away, the children made rude faces and noises and began chanting again.

Emunah had cared for a friend's frail son who was now quite the young scholar, able to read and write. She brought him odd bits of homespun rags and had him write words on them in lampblack—*Crook, Shyster, Hyena, Ogre, Leech*. These she pinned with thorns into the cracks in Ayah's garden wall. Whenever the judge walked from his home to his court, she followed, shouting, "Today Judge Ayah throws orphans into the street. . . . Sale today at Judge Ayah's court! Tear apart a will for 10 percent! Public drunk, prices on request! Come one, come all! Justice is never a problem!"

The judge's nerves jangled like harp strings. He couldn't eat or sleep or get the pesky crone out of his head.

After a week he finally burst from his house during his siesta serenade and shrieked at her: "Enough! Just *stop*! Before the day is out, the garrison will pay you in full, you satanic hag! You're driving me out of my mind!"

If such a hardhearted villain finally yields to confident and persistent faith, could we think our Father in heaven could resist the pleas of his faithful children?

Thoughts to Ponder

∾ *Patience.* Dante had the answer to our long-range frustrations. "In patience," he says, "we take possession of our souls." Our deep-rooted acceptance of competitiveness makes us miss the point of this parable: not that the old woman finally won judgment, but that she persisted. The answer isn't in the achieving; the answer's in the striving. In the going, we're already there.

There's something ennobling in persistence—something that makes us cheer Rocky when he gets up the fiftieth time, knowing he's going to be slammed down again. The Iraq veteran with dead legs who plays wheelchair basketball, a teacher relentlessly showing impaired kids how to tie their own shoes, the AIDS researcher going back into the lab day after day. The neighborhood organizer, the rebuilding-year coach, the recovering alcoholic. Such people don't pull in the big salaries, but they're the true heroes. They rarely get the spurious recognition of making the cover of *People* or being invited onto "The Tonight Show." Those spots are reserved for folks who accidentally happen to be physically beautiful, or can gyrate their pelvises and trash guitars, or can move an inflated pig bladder through eleven men down a big lawn with white stripes.

When it seems God has gone deaf to our pleas, we can think of Abraham Lincoln, Helen Keller, Bill Wilson, Rosa Parks, Dorothy Day, Nelson Mandela. Courage is not the foolhardiness that drives some to swim through sharks from Cuba to Florida. Genuine courage is coward's courage: "I *can't* keep going. . . . But I'll *try!*" Coward's courage strides toward the Auschwitz ovens, chin high. "You swine may be able to break my body, but you by God can't defile my soul."

~ *Spirit.* Paul wrote to the Romans: "For you did not receive a spirit that makes you a slave again to fear, but you received a spirit of sonship. And by him we cry, 'Abba, Father.' The Spirit himself testifies with our spirit that we are God's children. Now if we are children, then we are heirs—heirs of God and co-heirs with Christ, if indeed we share in his sufferings in order that we may also share in his glory" (Rom 8:15–17). Jesus said to his disciples: "I no longer call you servants. . . . Instead I have called you friends" (Jn 15:15).

God will rarely take the struggle away from us. He refused to do that for his only Son in his agony in the garden. The difference was in Jesus's *expectations* of what prayer can do: "Father, if you are willing, remove this cup from me; yet, not my will but yours be done." And his final prayer on the cross: "'Father, into your hands I commit my spirit" (Lk 23:46).

The painful question remains: Do I really *mean* that?

~ *Refusing to quit.* The great agnostic humanitarian Albert Camus sort of preempted the myth of Sisyphus to capture the only way to grasp a shred of dignity from the futility of pain in a godless universe. Sisyphus was condemned to roll a boulder up a mountain, but every time he gets it almost to the top and breathes a sigh of relief, the cursed thing rolls down again. Over and over he pushes the rock up, but Camus says that surely sometime Sisyphus must say, "Why not commit suicide and get it over with?" In that bleakest moment he sees where he can grasp some value to his suffering: "I *won't* quit!" Beyond patience, he finds value in sheer obstinacy. If the church can learn from a pagan like Plato, perhaps we can pick up some truth even from a modern unbeliever.

Richard Rohr, OFM, writes:

> We worship success. We quaintly believe we get what we deserve, what we work hard for and what we are worthy of. It is hard for Western people to think in any other way than in these categories.

After what we've already been given—for nothing we could have done to deserve it—it takes some *chutzpah* to keep believing God should feel impelled to give more.

∾ *God-given stubbornness.* Some Jewish sages claim that when we stand up to God, when we use the brains God gave us—not to knuckle under but to challenge him—God dances with delight! Because from the start God meant us to be *more* than docile sheep or clever apes. God wanted friends. Imagine! Our perseverance making God kick up his heels with joy! "Maybe . . . just maybe . . . they might understand what I made them for!"

6.

The Big-Hearted Grower
MATTHEW 20:1–16

*O*nce upon a time, at the end of a summer when the grape crop was extraordinarily plentiful, there was a vineyard owner named Zohar. His vines were so heavy with fruit that his own family and hired workers could not handle the harvest, so he went to the town well to hire more hands. When he got there, other fortunate growers had arrived to do the same. But that early in the day, there were so many the owners could pick the strongest and most eager. So Zohar hired as many as he could for the usual wage of a denarius a day and led them back to join his own crew.

But in the distance there were rumbles of thunder, and Zohar knew the whole harvest had to be finished in a single day, so back he went at midmorning for more hands. The dusty clothes on some of the newer ones showed they'd come some distance. Other vineyards faced the same need, so he said to the handful of men still loitering there, "Go to my vineyard, and I'll pay you what's fair." As the thunder edged closer, he went into the town again at midday and again midafternoon to hire anyone he could find. Finally, with still more vines to be picked he went out with only an hour of the workday left. There were still a few men there. "Why have you been lying around," Zohar said. "There's work for you!" They said, "We've been on the road most of the day. Anything you can give us, sir." So he sent them to his vineyard.

At last they had harvested all the grapes they could, and Zohar was filled with gratitude to God that they had saved almost everything. It was a fine harvest. So he told his overseer to call in the workers and pay them, starting with the last and working down to the first hired.

The ones who had worked only an hour got a denarius, a full day's pay. When the news dribbled back to those at the end of the line, they began to jostle one another and grin, sure that this guy was going to shell out big. If these late-coming bums got that much, for sure they'd get *ten* days' pay! But when they got to the table, they each got the same single denarius.

One of the first hired held his denarius in his fist and shook it at Zohar, who stood behind the table. "Wait just one minute," the worker snarled. "That last bunch worked just one lousy hour, an' you give 'em the same as us that's worked the whole day in this heat t' save your crop?"

"Friend," Zohar said, "I don't think you worked to save my crop. You worked because I said I'd pay you the usual day's wage. And I did."

"But listen here . . . "

"No, you listen. These last men had to come a long way. And—just like you—they have families to feed. I *want* to give them the same as you."

"But . . . "

"Have I done you any wrong? Are you saying I can't be generous with my own money?"

Hard as it is for a mind restricted to justice, the last are as good as the first.

Thoughts to Ponder

∽ *Unfair shares*. St. Paul writes:

Is there injustice on God's part? By no means! For
he says to Moses,

> "I will have mercy on whom I have
> mercy,
>   and I will have compassion on whom
>   I have compassion."

So it depends not on human will or exertion, but
on God who shows mercy. (Rom 9:14–16)

Apparently, there is no need for us to "*merit* to be
coheirs," since Jesus has already done that for us. Our
only contribution is accepting his generous kindness.

∽ *Earning value*. In the fourth century a heresy arose called Pelagianism, which insisted that we
not only can but must achieve salvation by our own
efforts. And despite its condemnation as heresy, that
conviction that we must not only *merit God's love*
but also *achieve salvation* by hauling ourselves up by
our own bootstraps is apparently still preached—and,
lamentably, also practiced by truly good people who
still feel inadequate to God's love.

The kindness of Christ is outrageous! We *can't*
merit it because it's ours for the taking! God loves us
as helplessly as a mother who continues to love her
child even on death row! Think of Yahweh in the book
of Hosea standing humbly, helplessly outside Israel's
whore house, waiting for Israel to come to her senses
and he can espouse her again (Hos 2).

St. Paul says the same: "Who will separate us from the love of Christ? Will hardship, or distress, or persecution, or famine, or nakedness, or peril, or sword?" (Rom 8:35).

The *Universal Catechism* states:

> The charity of Christ is the source in us of all our merits before God. Grace, by uniting us to Christ in active love, ensures the supernatural quality of our acts and consequently their merit before God and before men. The saints have always had a lively awareness that their merits were pure grace.

In other words, Christ is the Great Alchemist. His love for us transforms lead to gold.

     ∽ *Runaway allegory.* Many interpret those hired first as the Jews and wrongly conclude that the Jews are "less" than Christians. Part of the problem may be the usual translation, which is memorable because of the paradox and its catchy rhythm: "The last shall be first, and the first shall be last." But they seem to ignore the fact that, even if we are last, we're *welcome.* We may be at the end of the line, but there's plenty of room for us. We will "get in."

A similar silliness arises when people talk about "my place in heaven," as if monopolistic capitalism ruled there, too. Everybody in the parable gets the *same* reward. Can even God "weigh out" *degrees* of joy? Our joy will not be measured by our merits but by the size of the container we bring: the capacity of our souls for joy.

Even more troubling, caring parents often worry that their grown children are not going to "get into heaven" because they have stopped going to mass or they are living in sin. They are the same people who picture St. Peter at the heavenly gates "making a list, checking it twice." Jesus never did that with a sinner. Never. We ought never forget that Jesus himself declared that Abraham, Isaac, and Jacob are at the heavenly banquet—despite the fact they missed mass every single week of their long lives. Nor can we forget that Jesus forgave his fellow outlaw on the cross without pause or condition, and not because he confessed anything, but because he was kind.

God's ways are not our ways. Gandhi said, "I like your Christ, I do not like your Christians. Your Christians are so unlike your Christ."

∾ *The unworthy needy.* This parable might give second thoughts to practicing Christians who complain about migrant workers. Or scholarships for the less advantaged. In a race—say, at a summer camp—should a kid with a physical handicap be given a head start? If we play with a masters champion, should that person give us a handicap?

The workers hired early are like the prodigal son's older brother. They worked hard; there's no indication their work was less than satisfactory. But their complaint had nothing to do with justice. And in our honest moments, if we put ourselves in their sandals, most of us probably would admit we would feel exactly the same. At least a few coppers bonus for a long day. The resentment is unreasonable, given their agreement. It's a matter of feelings, not reason. The AA saying goes: "Resentment is like taking poison and hoping the other guy dies."

Instead of explaining Christ's death as atonement—justice, economics, ransom—Duns Scotus sees it as an ultimate act of God trying to show us how important we are to him. So: If God offered me a choice between justice from God or love, which would I ask for?

7.

The Timid Apprentice
MATTHEW 25:14–30

*O*nce upon a time, long before there were graduate schools for promising young men (and young women were learning how to humanize husbands and children), propertied parents often apprenticed their younger sons, who would inherit little, to men who had made their fortunes the hard way. For a price, of course. Such successful men would introduce boys (energized by the age-old motive *Strive or Starve*) to skills—and connections—that would assure their wives and children would have no need to learn the skills of beggary.

One such provider was an export-import trader named Batach, who also amplified his earnings with investments in local land speculation, building, and mining expeditions. His three apprentices were Amitz, Amin, and Shafan. Amitz had the easygoing confidence of a young man who knew he had been blessed and wanted to show gratitude to God and his parents. Amin was dutiful, humorless, but dependable. Shafan was the brightest, but his father had told him to come home rich or not at all. Thus he tended to be looking in all four directions at once.

When Batach left for an excursion around Mediterranean trading centers, he called each young man to his office and doled out a sum he thought commensurate with each boy's gifts. To Amitz he gave five talents, to Amin two, and to Shafan one. Now even a single talent was no paltry sum. It was seventy pounds of silver, equivalent to nine man-years' wages for a skilled worker. Therefore, Amitz received a bit over two million dollars, Amin about eight hundred thousand, and Shafan had no reason to be insulted by one talent, which amounted to nearly a half million.

Batach was gone longer than anyone expected, but then out of nowhere came news he would be home within days. The house servants bustled like a beehive to prepare, and the master arrived home from a string of international successes. After a day or two settling back in and monitoring his local enterprises, he called in his three apprentices for a reckoning.

Amitz came forward, trying his best to look humble, but he rolled up a chest laden with silver. He had speculated shrewdly in properties and start-up businesses. He said, "Sir, I've doubled the five talents you entrusted to me. Here are ten talents. And I thank you for the experience. It was frightening at times, but I enjoyed it."

"Fine, Amitz. Just fine. You deserve a percentage, lad. You'll go far. Excellent!"

Amin came forward, rolling another chest. "Sir," he said, "I did what I could. Here is your two talents back, and two talents more."

"Well done, Amin! You deserve a percentage, too! And bigger opportunities! You have a future, young man!"

Then Shafan lurched forward holding a dirt-stained headcloth that wrapped a heavy load, straining his arms. Seventy pounds of silver. "Sir," he said, laying his burden at Batach's feet. "I know you have a sharp eye, a man who values every shekel. I know what a fumbler I am, and I knew you would expect me to keep your investment in me safe. And to be sure I didn't lose a single coin, as soon as you gave me my talent, I wrapped it in this headcloth and buried it in the garden just outside my room. Here it is back safely. Not a single coin missing!"

Batach took in a heroic breath, and his face burned scarlet. "You gutless wretch," he growled. "Do you think my silver was hen's eggs to hatch by sitting on it? Didn't it even cross your mind to give it to a *banker*! So at the very least it would have gained interest from loans to foreigners?" He summoned his steward. "Take his talent and give it to Amitz. And as for him, throw him out on the road. There's no place for him here. Those who are ready to risk what they have for something better will prosper here. The mean-spirited will wither away."

Thoughts to Ponder

◦ *The metaphor.* This is obviously not a tale about money or the merits of venture capitalism. It demonstrates the spectrum between prudence and cowardice. I played with the Hebrew names: *batach* means "trust," *amitz* means "daring," *amin* means "trustworthy," and *shafan* means "wary." They represent the spectrum of the meanings of faith.

If the master in the story stands for God, Amitz and Amin seem to have a totally different God from Shafan's. The successful pair believed in a master who trusted them and expected them to trust *themselves*. Shafan's God, on the other hand, was not a father but an accountant. But the crux of the test was not the money but something less capable of "proof": confidence.

In our Christian education the heaviest attention was doctrinal—memorizing answers to questions that were neither pertinent nor even interesting. But Jesus seems never—never—to have taught that way. He worked for understanding and for trust. And—as in the case of Peter particularly—if understanding failed, then trust and big-heartedness were far more important.

The parable is an admonition against being overly cautious and scrupulous. Like the priest and Levite, like the elder brother, Shafan did nothing *wrong*. Pharisees smugly assumed righteousness because their slates were clean. But their hearts were empty. The same can happen when those in charge of worship are more meticulous about the historical and theological niceties than they are about stimulating the souls of those still clinging to the church.

The *moral* appended to the story is this: "To everyone who has, more will be given." That's sounds more like Ayn Rand than like the lilies-of-the-field Jesus who said that to find yourself, you have to lose yourself. What I suspect Jesus meant was that the more you risk giving yourself away, the richer you become. But it does demand a *risk*. Even the simple act of acknowledging that somebody is *there*, noticing a person, is a risk. Therefore, many people keep their eyes focused on the elevator numbers, immerse themselves in their smartphone lest they be intruded upon. We forget that our most precious friends were once strangers. Nine times out of ten, when we trust someone, he or she will reward your trust. Admittedly, one time out of ten we get scorched. So to avoid that one wound, we give up those nine potential friends. That's not even good economics!

∾ *Assessing talents.* The first truth to grasp is that each of us *is*, in fact, gifted. We spend far more time brooding over what we lack than dancing for joy over what we have, pouting that "the Master gave me one crummy talent." Someday, just for a change of pace, we can take some paper and list the talents we do have—what no Rwandan, for example, can ever hope for. Then we can start.

The second truth is to commit ourselves to exploiting those talents as diligently as a peasant woman milks the last drop out of her cow. But the analogy goes further than merely not wasting our talent. Talents grow with use and wither with disuse. Being Christian doesn't mean being "un-bad," like the third apprentice. Being Christian means making a difference with the talents we've been given, committing those talents, no matter the risk.

All of us want to be useful. But to be useful, we have to let ourselves be *used*.

∾ *Caution/cowardice?* According to the meek and gentle Jesus, this is what our Master will say to the falsely humble: "Throw that worthless servant outside, into the darkness, where there will be weeping and gnashing of teeth" (Mt 13:42). Not for any of the "hot sins" like lust, grand theft, murder. But unbending self-protectiveness. The sin of humility.

One look at a crucifix shows that the model of Christianity was not always cautious or even prudent. Indeed, some of us were brought up to be reserved, or we find introversion a more natural way of dealing with life. The unnerving truth is that Jesus was anything but reserved.

Dorothy Sayers undermines any delusion that Jesus was only meek and mild:

> The people who hanged Christ never, to do them justice, accused Him of being a bore—on the contrary; they thought Him too dynamic to be safe. It has been left for later generations to muffle up that shattering personality and surround Him with an atmosphere of tedium. We have very efficiently pared the claws of the Lion of Judah, certified Him "meek and mild," and recommended Him as a fitting household pet for pale curates and pious old ladies. To those who knew Him, however, He in no way suggested a milk-and-water person; they objected to Him as a dangerous firebrand. . . . He was emphatically not a dull man in His human lifetime, and if He was God, there can be nothing dull about God either. But He had "a daily beauty in His life that made us ugly," and officialdom felt that the established order of things would be more secure without Him. So they did away with God in the name of peace and quietness.

∾   There's one last kicker to the Parable of the Talents. Guess what you get for a job well done. More jobs. But Tennyson's *Ulysses* answers that:

> How dull it is to pause, to make an
>   end,
> To rust unburnished, not to shine in
>   use!
> As though to breathe were life!

8.

The Crafty Steward
LUKE 16:1–13

*O*nce upon a time, when obedience was more valued than creativity, there was a very rich man named Ethan who owned a large plantation he had divided into tenant farms. Families who had a run of bad luck or poor choices and had lost their hereditary farms had little choice but to become his clients—sharecroppers who farmed their assigned five-acre plots from dawn to dusk and gave the landlord an agreed-upon percentage of their harvests in the late summer or early fall. Ethan was tough and gruff but reasonable, a man who could tell just by the feel of it if a coin had been shaved round the edge. But he'd never in his life kicked a balky mule.

His steward, Orem, was a freedman, quick-witted and lively. He had a reputation of being partial to the underdog, occasionally giving breaks under the table to a man whose son had run off or whose daughter was shockingly with child. He juggled the books awhile till the tenant paid it back. This did not sit well with tenants who also wanted a break but had no reason to justify it. So the discontented sharecroppers told Ethan that Orem was embezzling his money. And

Ethan simply assumed his steward was creeping off to the city and living the high life on the sly.

The news got round the farms, and one farmer he'd helped warned Orem, so when Ethan said he wanted to go over the rolls the following week, Orem went cold. "There's been talk, Orem. If it's true, you better start explaining."

Well, at least the master hadn't mentioned the magistrate. Or the jailer. "What can I do?" he asked himself. "I'm too spindly to dig, too proud to beg." So he thought and thought and thought. Then it came to him. He dug out the rolls with the original leases he had worked out with the tenants, and he began with a knife and a piece of pumice to erase all the amounts. Then he summoned each of the debtors—even those who had turned him in to the boss.

They were all subsistence farmers, and a wonderful year meant little more than not starving. And this had been a so-so year, where every measure probably meant an old grandpa's life. To each one Orem said, "Remind me. What's your yearly tariff?"

Tears in his eyes, one said, "A 100 measures of oil."

"See? It's worn off the parchment. Sit down, and—in your own hand—write 50."

The tenant's hand was shaking so hard he could hardly write the numbers, and he couldn't get breath to gasp his thanks. His whole life had just come back to him.

To the next, one who hated him, Orem said, "Could you remind me how much you owe?"

The angry tenant growled, "A 100 measures of wheat." He sat, steaming.

"See? Your line there where the number was has faded. Sit down and write 80."

The sharecropper's face twisted into an even deeper scowl of disbelief.

"Go on," Orem said. "Just write in the new number."

And so it went. Even with those who had hated him and reported him to Ethan.

Everyone was jubilant. So, of course, they gathered to celebrate in the village square. And they even invited Ethan, the master.

When Ethan strode in, the whole square fell silent. News had spread round that this gift of a whole new life probably had been news to him. It *couldn't* have been without his approval. Could it? Good old Ethan! What a master! Now, who could deny him anything? Anything reasonable, that is. Ethan crooked his finger at Orem, who came up to him, hardly breathing.

"You scalawag," Ethan snorted, shaking his head. "You figured every measure of wheat was a slab of their flesh and every jar of oil was their life's blood. You ninny! Do you think I have less of a heart than you? Bravo! Initiative like that is the best obedience."

And both farmers and villagers rejoiced even more because they had the best master and steward on God's whole green earth and for some distance beyond.

This steward, Orem, was dishonest—wasn't he? In his head he was cunning as a serpent, but in his heart he was as guileless as a dove.

Thoughts to Ponder

 ∾ *Contracts*. Two processes were used by scribes in preparing palimpsests, that is, reusing materials previously written on. The writing was washed off with a sponge and the parchment smoothed when dry by rubbing with pumice stone. Or entire lines were scraped off with a sharp blade and the surface rubbed smooth with pumice stone or a polishing tool.

~ *Judgment.* Why is it not surprising that the boss—and probably any listeners—simply assumes if someone is embezzling, the person *must* be doing it to live life in the fast lane? Before passing judgment on Orem, calling him—as has been done for two thousand years—"the wicked steward . . . unjust . . . unrighteous . . . conniving . . . self-seeking," it's well to remember that during Jesus's entire public life the official churchmen accused *him* of deserving all those negative adjectives. Also, recall that Jesus was condemned to death by two different courts, one for blasphemy and the other for civil disobedience.

The only motive the text gives for the steward's larcenous kindness: "So that, when I am dismissed as manager, people may welcome me into their homes." True enough. But which of us has ever done anything—good or bad—from a single unmixed motive?

Because Jesus clearly praises a clever thief, this is the thorniest of the parables. It has been called the problem child of parable exegesis and has created a jungle of explanations. And I make bold to conjure up yet another. I tried to make it at least remotely Christian.

One suggestion is Jesus disengages the rascal's dishonesty from his foresight, implicitly disapproving of the one and lauding the other. Another more dramatic suggestion simply separates verses 1–8 (the story) from verses 9–13 (the lesson) and claims it was added later. This answer appeals even to some major critics. Jeremias suggests the early writers converted the "lesson" from a warning to make preparations for the endtimes to "a direction [to Christians] for the right use of wealth, and a warning against unfaithfulness." Yet another thinks the rogue steward risked "everything on the quality of mercy he has already experienced from his master," while others imagine he'd been gouging them all along and now gave back his inflated commissions. Yet another believes the real hero of the parable is not the steward but the *master*, who was generous to his cheating steward. The wise person puts total trust in the loving Lord and the riches of his grace. Like the prodigal son with his father. The difference between Simon Peter, who trusted Jesus could forgive him, and Judas Iscariot, who was certain no one could.

    ~ *Possible intentions.* No matter who has the "right" take on the story, anyone can draw a lesson from it. First, we could get a few nifty ideas from crooks. Persuasive salesmanship is a neutral skill; the key is what the purveyor is offering. Those in charge of evangelization should learn from the hucksters of Madison Avenue the arts of persuasion that render people susceptible to a product they find initially unattractive. Second, money itself isn't bad; it can effect good. Third, Jesus himself was welcomed by just such conniving outsiders and crooks. Why did he agree to consort with them? Fourth, the story can speak of convincing ways to use a different kind of wealth.

Luke (the only one with this story) was writing for learned aristocrats, so he spends a lot of time talking about what's more important than money. At least one can say this story, in D. P. Seccombe's words, "leads the wise disciple to use his possessions in the service of the needy." Not just possessions, but wits. The steward is a rascal, but a wonderfully clever rascal.

Along that line, most of us join a millennially long line of fascinated listeners who enjoy the rapscallion heroes of uncounted tales of "angels with dirty faces": Robin Hood, Scheherazade, the Artful Dodger, Br'er Rabbit, Tom Jones, Becky Sharp, Moll Flanders, Huck Finn and Tom Sawyer, Scarlett O'Hara, the Music Man, Princess Leia, Han Solo. Will "puritans" allow Jesus to be playful? He seems to have delighted in verbal byplay with the Samaritan woman at the well and the Syro-Phoenician woman who told him even puppies could eat what children spilled. Not to mention calling the fumbling Peter "Rocky."

   Praising duplicity? Scripture describes the master's reaction: "His master commended the dishonest [*adikias*] manager because he had acted shrewdly [*phronimos*]." No escape from the meaning of *adikias* as "fraudulent." Nor does the original story allow for any hint that the steward was acting with his employer's permission or approval. But *phronimos* allows a bit more leeway—which the reader will note that, in my Jesuitical way, I took every advantage of here. The thesaurus offers three different clusters of synonyms for *shrewd*, like *cunning* (which in turn yields sixty-six more), *intelligent* (with eighteen more) and *knowing* (twenty-five more), including a range from *insidious* and *Machiavellian* to *diplomatic* and *perceptive* and even *wise*.

This parable, spoken "to his disciples," can also be read as enjoining the early Christians to be shrewd in avoiding their Jewish and pagan pursuers and death. This is not like the Hale-Bopp Comet cult craving suicide for a quicker trip to eternal life. (Google "Jesuit equivocation.")

Verse 9 is the fishbone in the throat. Luke shows Jesus, the narrator, giving the final interpretation of the story's purpose: "And I tell you, make friends for yourselves by means of dishonest wealth so that when it is gone, they may welcome you into the eternal homes." Maybe "corrupting" or "deceptive" wealth might be more fitting.

That doesn't say money is bad. It's a good servant, but a bad master. Like cleverness, money's a means, not an end. What Jesus is commissioning us to do, I think, is to use canny imagination in service of a nobler end: enlightening and enlivening those too willing to settle for mere survival. We're sent to wake them up to a more profound way of being human. Not only kids just emerging from total self-centeredness, but adults for whom confession is now no longer any more operative than feeling guilty for disobeying their parents' ideas of acceptable behavior.

What do shrewd advertisers do with a product they believe in, but to which potential buyers show utter indifference? They bend every persuasive skill to create an awareness of their "need" for the product. In the Great Depression, how many knew they "needed" a deodorant? They had far more important needs, like hungry kids. The poor are "blessed" because they know what's truly important: food, clothing, shelter, and work. Refugees and immigrants know, too: being alive, family, hope.

Finally, I can't help admiring that conniving manager. It seems Jesus did, too! He admires *initiative*—which in this case means not just pushing the envelope but lopping off the top. I got a lot of pressure, from first grade through graduate school, to imitate the gentleness of doves, but I can't recall a single even tentative suggestion to emulate the wily skills of the serpent. Yet—in my fifty years of trying to "sell" the gospel to teenagers and adults—I've found my devi-ousness and imagination far—far!—more useful than meek conformity. No salesperson ever succeeded by being a bashful automaton.

9.

Truly Rich, Truly Poor

LUKE 16:19–31

*O*nce upon a time, long ago, when the rich got richer and the poor got poorer, there was an outrageously rich man named Dives. His long-lived mother, a woman of beauty unwithered in a lifetime, had married no fewer than six times, each time enjoying a larger inheritance, accumulating wealth enough to dispel any suggestion of black widowhood. And at her lamentable death, the whole megillah fell to her disgracefully spoiled only child, Dives.

Dives lived a life as full of luxurious distractions and devoid of discomfort or drawbacks as the emperor himself. His doting mama had guaranteed her son would never lack for any pleasure or ever be upset. Any slightest hint of sickness or old age or death or deformity was forbidden from the family compound—absolutely.

All day Dives lounged in purple velvet on goose-down pillows while peach-faced girls plucked delicately on tiny harps and sang lilting melodies. Or, if that grew tedious, limber young boys defied gravity and expectations in gymnastic feats. Or, more rarely, old men who had given their lives to learning explained for him the simpler insights of the lesser Greek philosophers. At the rare times Dives was needed outside the compound, he was carried in a sedan chair enclosed in heavy draperies, lest his equilibrium be in any slightest way jostled.

Meanwhile, at the great iron gate to his mansion above the cool lake of Tiberias, a leper named Lazarus hunched in a heap, holding up his begging bowl to important visitors as their sedan chairs lurched by up the road, hoping to convince the wealthy master to invest in some venture.

Lazarus was utterly repellant, covered with running sores that masterless dogs came and licked at their leisure. Day after day, Dives's servants tried to bully the beggar away, but they were terrified to touch him, lest they be infected. The best they could do was yell and hurl rocks at him till they tired of it. He refused to crawl away.

Now no one—rich or poor—is able to elude the one certain fact of life: death. And both Lazarus and Dives died within hours of each other. Dives went one way, Lazarus the other.

With a reversal the wise come to expect, wretched Lazarus was wafted outside the wearying clutches of Time into the glory of paradise, swathed in silk, couched near a bubbling fountain in a sunlit grove of flowering trees. His horrid flesh was now firm and sleek as a child's, and his table companion was none other than Father Abraham, grandsire of the Hebrew people. Lazarus could hardly contain his joy.

The place where Dives found himself was just as unexpected. No harps in fragile hands, no boys passing among the couches with chilled wine and sugared almonds. Instead, a dreary village square, hot and airless. People slouched disdainfully through the vast, featureless open space, sneering and snarling at nothing—or everything. A Nowhere.

Then, immured within that unacceptable nightmare, Dives had an upsetting vision. More than a vision—a garden more real than reality that he could see but never enter. And there, lounging on a couch next to a pool was Father Abraham! And on the next couch, draped in rich royal purple, a man he thought he vaguely remembered. The man's face came into focus through the brilliant haze. The disgusting leper! Dives had seen him once through the curtains of his palanquin. No!

But it was. Now he remembered. The leper's name was Lazarus.

Lazarus's hand trailed in the waters ruffled by the fountain, and red-golden fish nibbled delicately at his healed fingertips. Dives could see it, clear as clear, as if he were really standing right next to them. He looked at Father Abraham's serene face, smiling at the healed leper.

"Father Abraham?" Dives whispered.

Abraham looked up, as if he had heard a buzz. He squinted. "Yes? Speak up. I can hardly hear you. You're so very far away."

"Oh, Father, pity! I'm so wretched here. So lonely. Lost. And the thirst. Pity! Order Lazarus to come and just let the water from his hand drip into my parched mouth. I'm in agony."

"Ah, my child," Abraham sighed, "it's not possible. There is an impassable abyss between you and us. Just as there was all your life. What you thought was life was really upside down. By the will of God, you were privileged, despite the smallness of your soul, and Lazarus had a miserable life, which he rose above with trust and dignity. You were so distracted."

With the profoundest of sighs, Dives realized he had missed all further chances. "Then, Father Abraham, please—send this man who lived well all his life. Let him tell my friends and relatives this truth. Let him warn them. Make them see it. Otherwise, they'll end up in godforsaken torment, too."

"Have they read Job," Abraham asked.

"Yes, of course, Father, but . . . "

"All their lives," Abraham said, as the vision began ever so slowly to fade, "they've had Moses. They've had uncounted prophets, one after another, telling them the truth—about widows, orphans, aliens."

"But Father," Dives shouted at the weakening apparition, "*wait*! My brothers have seen that man. Outside my gate! He can be *proof* to them!"

Nothing left but a whisper. "If they refuse all the voices of God's chosen messengers, voices they've heard for a lifetime, they'll be deaf even to one come back from the dead."

And at that, for pampered Dives, began the eternal silence.

Thoughts to Ponder

ᴑ *Editing the story*. For two reasons I've tweaked the parable. One motive was to give some credence to the extent of Dives's wealth (which meant changing his "five brothers" to his "relatives"). The other was to link this story across human experience to the story of Gautama Siddhartha, who became The Buddha. Siddhartha's father had pampered and protected his son so in adulthood he would choose to be king in luxury and power and foreswear sanctity—wholeness.

My primary motive for harmonizing the Dives and Siddhartha stories was to dissuade well-meaning "helicopter parents," who guard their young from the slightest unpleasantness, like a failing grade they really deserve. Such lethal "love" protects them not only from momentary upset but from adulthood. More pertinently here, it guarantees they will never value as a model a felon like Jesus, exhausted on a crucifix for others.

My further motive was to show that the rock-bottom truths of human value and purpose are the same no matter where in the world and into what religious tradition we search. The Golden Rule—"Do unto others as you would have others do unto you"—is not an exclusive truth of Christianity. We find it echoed—often word for word—in every human philosophy ever assembled. It is not a matter of religion but of human survival.

The truth remains true, no matter what the source.

∾ *Surplus.* In Hebrew culture a God-given surplus *ought* to be shared, as witness the so-called lost parables: lost coin, lost sheep, lost son. In each story the burst of good fortune demands a celebration. Which is the meaning of *Eucharist.* To act otherwise was to be an ingrate, greedy. This constitutive element of Christianity sits uncomfortably with many when the subjects of immigration and welfare arise.

∾ *Paradox.* When all's said and done, Lazarus ends in the spot of honor up center where Dives used to sit. This role reversal in every scripture story since Genesis has become inevitable. And it is the basis for folktales ever since (and a great deal of humor). Consider Cinderella or Jack and the Beanstalk, as unlikely as a girl from a back-country village becoming mother of the Messiah or an apostate fisherman chosen to be the first pope.

However, despite a lifetime of such Old Testament stories, despite even the evident unpleasantness and abrupt change of death, Dives *still* doesn't "get it." Like the Pharisees, he presumes Abraham is his father—by the mere accident of bloodlines. He still looks down on Lazarus as a menial—"Order Lazarus," he says—meant to serve him. Wise Father Abraham knows even resurrection will not penetrate Dives's culpable ignorance.

Along that same line, remember those who had spent three years, 24/7, with Jesus, who took in his words as naturally as they smelled his sweat, experienced *firsthand* the staggering resurrection of Jesus. And yet—can you believe it?—their *very* last question, the instant before Jesus's ascension, was: "Lord, is this the time when you will restore the kingdom to Israel?" (Acts 1:6). After all they'd gone through, the only thing they cared about was whether this was the payoff moment when they would become Big Shots. Jesus must have taken a deep breath and wondered what was keeping that elevator!

We're in excellent company if we still misread Jesus. Here is the justification for service projects: to unlearn privilege. This parable is not a moral dictum, just a restating of the Beatitudes and Magnificat.

~ *"Making it."* At least in some ways the Parable of Dives supports what most of us have learned about salvation. For many, it means sneaking into heaven. My mom used to say, "Pray, Billy, that I can just manage to grab the doorsill of heaven with my fingernails." It seemed close to unfair that the gangland legend Dutch Schultz *just* managed to get the last rites and squeak his lousy soul into heaven, the gates pinching his heels. Just one more example of the ubiquitous "economic metaphor," God defined by bean counters. As if God were an IRS agent foiled by some swine getting his income-tax envelope stamped at 11:59:59. Death as a Hail Mary pass into the celestial end zone.

How sad that image is. A God directly counter to the Good Shepherd, who entrusts ninety-nine sheep to another shepherd in order to trace down one dumb stray, not to mention the father of the prodigal who embraces and kisses his renegade child *before* the kid can even apologize!

The God who's supervised the death and rebirth of supernovas and uncountable species—and who demonstrated on Calvary the impermanence of death—is hardly likely to find that even Death limits access to salvation.

For a more lenient understanding of heaven and hell, see C. S. Lewis, *The Great Divorce*. In it everybody gets a second chance after the flat EKG. In defiance of Dante's operatic imagination, the dead are in a snappish, nasty Grey Town that they can leave anytime they choose, if only they surrender their narcissism. If they do, the Grey Town has been purgatory. If they refuse, it becomes hell. Lewis bases his reimagining on Milton's Lucifer: "Better to reign in hell than serve in heaven."

James Stephens's poem, "In the Fullness of Time," softens the harshness of the parable:

> On a rusty iron throne
> Past the furthest star of space
> I saw Satan sit alone,
> Old and haggard was his face;
> For his work was done and he
> Rested in eternity.

And to him from out the sun
Came his father and his friend
Saying, now the work is done
Enmity is at an end:
And he guided Satan to
Paradises that he knew.

Gabriel without a frown,
Uriel without a spear,
Raphael came singing down
Welcoming their ancient peer,
And they seated him beside
    One who had been crucified.

That is a God I find much easier to worship than
the one I met as a child.

10.

The Hidden Treasure
MATTHEW 13:44

*O*nce upon a time, long, long ago, when people still thanked God for what today we call good luck, there was a day laborer named Eban. As the third son of a landless, luckless father, Eban had little to support himself, his wife, and his firstborn son—only his wits, his willingness to work, the sweet-tempered mule named Jethro gifted to him by an uncle, and the tough plow Eban had spent a whole winter shaping from half of a rock-hard oak stump, then faced with metal from two discarded Roman shields he'd charmed from the armorer of the town garrison. Then clever Eban borrowed the Roman's tools and his forge to shape and sharpen the blade.

Eban and Jethro rented their services with plow and chains to farms to yank up big rocks and stumps, pull down shacks, haul carcasses to market on a sledge. This day, at the behest of some foreign real estate agent, they were carving a long groove in the rich black soil of some absentee landlord. This had once been a flourishing plantation tended by scores of slaves, but the owners had run afoul of Rome. Something to do with two sons and an assassination. The family fled with nothing but the clothes they stood in—consoled with funds in various banks. Now, after years of parceling and passing from hand to hand, this new Roman hired Eban and Jethro to make the plot more attractive. It was good land but too small to attract big spenders.

Eban passed the time praying aloud, Jethro at times adding a snort in Amen. The reverie snapped when the plowshare snagged with a clank against a large flat rock just below the sod. Eban grabbed his spade and peeled away the weeds. Not so big, but too large to lift. He wrapped the chains around the rock, clucked to Jethro, and the docile mule popped the rock and dragged it to the footpath. Eban upended it, leaving it for the new owner to do with as he pleased.

He unwrapped the chains, took them back to weight down the blade again, and took up the reins. But a glint from the shallow pit where the rock had been caught his eye. He pulled the reins and said, "Well, looky here, Jethro."

Eban squatted, reached into the depression, and picked up a shiny silver denarius. A full day's pay! Old, but as good as any newly minted piece! The face incised on the coin must be some emperor's, but the words meant nothing since Eban had never learned Roman writing. It should have burned his fingers— the graven image—but the fragile weight of the silver warmed his heart.

Clay shards clustered where the coin had been. Eban pawed them away and unearthed the oblong flanks of an amphora, cracked open by the plow point. And the fat-bellied thing was filled with coins. And carved red and green stones in shiny settings. And some gold pieces.

And it was all *his*.

He struggled to get a breath!

He picked up the broken pot; the contents tumbled from the long broken neck of the clay amphora like pebbles in a rainbow stream. Eban sank back on his heels and fought to regain ownership of his heart and lungs. Jethro nosed him, wondering what all the fuss was about.

"Oh, my good God," Eban groaned. "Oh!"

Years ago, when the original family had fled, it had buried the wealth too cumbrous and dangerous to carry, marking it with the flat rock. But that family never came back. Leaving it for the new owner.

Eban knelt there a long time trying his best to thank the Most Holy.

For nearly a week Eban and his wife scurried from broker to broker, selling everything they owned. Even the painfully wrought plow. But not Jethro. Together, they approached the Roman agent. The foreigner was skeptical at the slimness of their offer, but he yielded when Eban signed a note to guarantee the agent one-third of the next year's crop. Which the agent felt no need to declare when he sent the purchase price to the absentee landlord.

And Eban and his family and Jethro began life again in a totally transformed world.

Thoughts to Ponder

~ *Kingdom*. Whatever that word meant to Jesus, this parable makes it clear that Jesus believed it is the *ultimate* value. "What does it profit them if they gain the whole world, but lose themselves?" (Lk 9:25). The kingdom is a value worth giving up everything else to be worthy of. (Below we consider how even using the word *attain* for possessing the kingdom is a dangerous misuse of words.)

The kingdom encompasses all that Jesus Christ *means*: the fusion of divinity and humanity who embraced imperfection to become our liberator from all fear of sin and death. He is *the* way, *the* truth, *the* life. St. Paul says it in at least six places: "Be imitators of me as I am an imitator of Christ Jesus." The values manifested in all Jesus said and did should be the touchstones of anything that calls itself Christian: open-minded, open-hearted, open-handed welcome, forgiveness, healing, and starting over. *No one* is "lost" unless he or she chooses to be.

Therefore, what this parable implies—but I have never heard amplified—is that unless we have evaluated what the Christian message means and reacted with the same unqualified jubilation Eban felt holding his crock of coins and jewels, unless the meaning of Jesus leaves us *jumping for joy* like a reprieved convict, we haven't truly found the kingdom yet! All those catechisms and theology classes and homilies failed to ignite in us what Jesus set aflame in *his* disciples.

~ *Buying the kingdom.* It seems a small thing, but the element in this story that has had a very broad, painful effect on Christian understanding for two thousand years and across the spectrum from the cleverest theologians to ordinary Christians in the pew is that the fortunate plowman has to *buy* the field in order to have a right to the treasure. At its worst, this conviction is a heresy called Pelagianism, which held that we must *achieve* the kingdom through prayers, masses, self-denial. We have to *purchase* it with effort and

self-control. In apparent defiance of liturgical watch-
dogs, that belief is voiced without apparent challenge
in the Second Eucharistic Prayer:

> Have mercy on us all, we pray, that with the
> blessed Virgin Mary, Mother of God, with the
> blessed Apostles, and all the Saints who have
> pleased you throughout the ages, we may *merit*
> to be co-heirs to eternal life, and may praise and
> glorify you through your Son, Jesus Christ.

That is what Jesus did *for* us. We simply cannot
merit what we already have. But as result of that mis-
understanding, many good people simply cannot accept that they are loved. It's a gift! Grace given despite
our inadequacy! That's what makes it so wonderful!
But so many overly rational people try to make God
as small souled as they themselves are.

　　～ *Economics—Again*. We can too easily become prisoners of our metaphors, forgetting they are
approximations. When we say "Alfie is a pig," the
listener gets a better idea than before of what Alfie is
like. But the metaphor isn't a point for point *equiva-
lence*. We can't extend it to say Alfie has a curly tail
and cloven feet.

　　Unfortunately—because of the preconceptions of his
audience about money as the final determinant of human value—even Jesus's specially chosen seminarians
misheard him. Today, because of our own unexamined
values, we can garble worldly values and otherworldly
values. As a result dedicated Christians can unwittingly
imitate Pharisees and treat their "treasure" in heaven
exactly as they treat their bank balances and purgatory
like a debtors' prison from which they have to ransom

their loved ones. Some make it a mission to "pay off the debt" of those souls who have nobody who loves them and can pray for them—as if God had suspended his love.

Jesus often compares finding the kingdom to finding something materially valuable: the parables of the talents, wicked tenants, mustard seed, bountiful harvests, feeding thousands, leaven, unmerciful servant, laborers in the vineyard, rich fool. But they're symbols, not photographs.

It's hard to think of any analogy that would carry the same weight. As a result, even now, even after Vatican II, the *Catechism* (1031) declares we have to pay off that debt in purgatory. The sin can be forgiven here by confession and penance (*reatus culpae:* guilt), but we still have to pay damages (*reatus poenae:* reparation). Which makes the "Official God" as cripplingly vindictive as the Allies were to Germany after World War I. This is directly contradictory to the father of the prodigal son and to Jesus's unvarying magnanimity dealing one-on-one with sinners.

∾ *Spiritual treasure.* Draining the parable of all material fixations, there is a spiritual meaning here echoed in Jesus's statement to Nicodemus (Jn 3) that to gain the kingdom, we have to be born again. Clearly, Jesus didn't mean return to material gestation. But he did mean to start over—which is a hallmark of God's desires since the Big Bang.

Nicodemus was asked to *unlearn* all he'd rigorously learned. To *unlearn* his conviction Israel was still Yahweh's exclusive conduit. He had to learn a clean slate was no substitute for an empty heart. And we have to unlearn any doctrine that says we have to "*merit* to be coheirs to eternal life."

In order to understand Jesus we've got to become a child again—susceptible to enchantment, able to see a castle in an empty cardboard box, a princess in a checkout girl, God in a carpenter. We have to accept a God completely different from the God those well-meaning teachers told us was totally opposed to worldlings, sinners, the Sopranos, gays. God's ways are totally opposed to "the world's" *values,* not to the world's *people.* God is against ransoms, against quid pro quos, against penances to erase sins. Right here, Jesus said God *loves* the world—helplessly. God sent his only Son to die—horribly—*not* to pay off some godawful debt (to himself!), but to demonstrate how to stand up to suffering and death with dignity and faith. He died in order to rise, to prove death *isn't* the end. If only our teachers spent more time on that instead of on the weaknesses that allegedly "demanded" his death. The kingdom would be a treasure.

 ～ *Dishonesty.* The same penny-pinching minds bring up the moral issue in a parable obviously intended to be spiritual rather than fiducial. "If the plowman were honorable, he'd have declared his discovery to the land agent before offering to buy the plot."

When Eban bought the plot, he bought everything in the plot—even all the items the agent was unaware of, like the weeds, worms, and whatever water lurked under the surface.

Anyone benighted by such scruples should be compelled to go home and willfully cut off the warning labels from their pillows and mattresses. And fearlessly tell their neighbors about it. Scruples are so un-Jesus.

11.

Two Men Praying
LUKE 18:9–14

*O*nce upon a time, very long ago, when people were unafraid to pray right out loud, two men found themselves in the Great Temple in Jerusalem at the time of the afternoon sacrifice.

Now, the Temple was one of the largest buildings in the world. It covered thirty-five acres, seven times as large as the Roman Forum. At the center of two enormous cloistered courtyards was the Holy of Holies where the spirit of Yahweh dwelt among them, its curtained entrance guarded by two outer chapels, the outermost allowing purified Hebrew females, the middle one only Hebrew males. But strict rules limited all others to the vast outer courts. Further, all those judged unclean were restricted to the area just inside the Eastern Gate.

On the steps of the outermost chapel stood a prosperous city landlord named Hezekiah. His hands were pressed flat against the wall next to the doorway to the outer chapel, forehead, shrouded in his prayer shawl, pressed against the cool stone. He was a Pharisee, a man whose neighbors acknowledged was everything the Law intended a Jew to be. Which was precisely what had brought him to this holy place: to thank the

Lord for the assurance of his divine favor, the confidence that comes from having done everything he had been taught was required of a good man—and more.

He mumbled aloud verses from the psalms the inspired King David seemed to have written for precisely someone of Hezekiah's good fortune:

> "Vindicate me, O Lord,
>   for I have walked in my integrity. . . .

> "I do not sit with the worthless,
>   nor do I consort with hypocrites;
> I hate the company of evildoers,
>   and will not sit with the wicked." (Ps
>   26:1, 4–5)

His heart so swelled with gratitude that he paused to get his breath, then continued:

> "Do not sweep me away with sinners,
>   nor my life with the bloodthirsty,
> those in whose hands are evil devices,
>   and whose right hands are full of
>   bribes.

> "But as for me, I walk in my integrity;
>   redeem me, and be gracious to me.
> My foot stands on level ground;
>   in the great congregation I will bless
>   the Lord." (Ps 26:9–12)

There was some hubbub over to his right among the rabble of the unworthy by the Eastern Gate. It distracted him from his prayer. To his astonishment, he saw among the unclean his own tax assessor, Tikvah.

How could a gouging crook like that dare to enter this holy place? Even over there? Like a snake in a baby's cradle. It moved him to further grateful prayer, something like this:

> "Thank you, my ever-gracious Lord, that I can hold my head up among the rest of men. Except for the sustenance that comes from loving your Law, I'd be as disgusting in your eyes as Tikvah over there. The hypocrisy of his daring to be here! Thank you that I have the conviction to fast not once a year but twice a week, that instead of hoarding for myself and my family and my business, I faithfully give a tenth of all I earn and all I possess to the Law that bids us care for your Temple and for those too slothful to care for themselves and their too-many children."

Meanwhile, crammed among the outcasts, Tikvah, the tax collector, tried to stand tall, but it seemed unfitting for such a man as himself. He, too, prayed aloud words from Psalms, handed down by great King David.

> "Out of the depths I cry to you, O
>   Lord.
>   Lord, hear my voice!
> Let your ears be attentive
>   to the voice of my supplications!
>
> "If you, O Lord, should mark iniqui-
>   ties,
>   Lord, who could stand?
> But there is forgiveness with you. . . .

> "I wait for the Lord, my soul waits,
>   and in his word I hope;
> my soul waits for the Lord
>   more than those who watch for the
>   morning." (Ps 130:1–6)

He hung his head and scoured the tears away with his fist and continued something like this:

> "How do I dare impose myself on a place like this, with good people who struggle to live decent lives? Worse—how do I dare appear in *your* house? But that one little boy. When I put the family out on the road. That boy. With the tears in his big eyes and snot running from his nose. Screaming at me! 'Jackal! Vulture!' he screamed. Who taught him that. My Lord? You?
>   "Yes. You. Lord, have mercy. I am a sinner. Without your mercy, I'm abandoned."

Thoughts to Ponder

~ *Caricature.* As written, the parable lends itself too easily to oversimplification. If the two men were so blindly single-minded in exaggerating their accomplishment and their faults, neither would find much need or purpose to be in the Temple at all.

~ *Pharisees* weren't conniving villains from biblical films. Most were men who genuinely wanted to find and do the will of God. In fact, some warned Jesus that Herod was out to get him (Lk 17:31), and not all who came asking questions had axes to grind. Granted, the gospel writers, suffering fiercely prejudicial treatment from synagogues as a renegade sect, chose words to characterize the Pharisees that make us uneasy today. Jesus calls them "rapacious" (Lk 11:39) and "money lovers" (Lk 16:14). Matthew 23 is a textbook of indictments.

The Law appointed one fast in the year, the Day of Atonement, but the Pharisees also fasted on Mondays and Thursdays each week. It would be petty to criticize this man for doing more than the Law asked. What makes him suspect is that he feels compelled to mention it himself—and to a God one assumes is already aware of it. He confesses not his sins but his virtues.

I felt a pang of greater tolerance than ever before when I thought of this man while remembering my childhood understanding of a "good Catholic man." Back in the 1930s, he unhesitatingly attended novenas, rosary crusades, wore a scapular or Miraculous Medal, belonged to the Knights of Columbus and the *Catholic War Veterans*, scrupulously fasted even from accidentally swallowed toothpaste water before communion, and made a confession weekly. We were nearly as fastidious. I don't recall anyone being pompous about it. It was just routine.

But if charity fails to dispose us to greater nuance, justice surely must. It's as gratuitous to use the broad brush on "all Pharisees" as it is for "all Germans . . . all blacks . . . all Catholics."

✑ *Tax collectors* seem to have been—in most cases—worthy of the obloquy dumped on them, social vermin. There was a Roman income tax, import/export taxes, crop taxes (1/10 of grain; 1/5 of wine, fruit, olive oil), sales tax, property tax, emergency tax, entry and exit taxes, and on and on. As a class, tax collectors were presumed to be dishonest and classified by scholars with murderers and bandits, untrustworthy witnesses.

It might not be totally inaccurate to compare them to modern organized criminals who sell "protection" and act as loan sharks with a high "vig." They were equivalently highway robbers and collaborators; they had no civil rights. The flaw in the analogy is that they were not only tolerated but licensed by church and state.

Therefore, this crook's vindication by Jesus was a shock. The same was true of making a renegade Samaritan a hero, praising the woman known as a sinner when she burst in on a dinner given for him by Simon the Pharisee (Lk 7), indirectly faulting the elder brother for refusing to love his prodigal brother, forgiving the adulteress the elders were ready to stone. When people ask if God can forgive Hitler or suicide bombers or abortionists, I'm stuck not only with the unerringly consistent practice of Jesus—not to mention the persistently faithful Yahweh to persistently errant Israel. This God seems incapable of a grudge—provided we want forgiveness.

In Luke 3, after John the Baptist called Pharisees a brood of vipers, we read, "Even tax collectors came to be baptized, and they asked him, 'Teacher, what should we do?' He said to them, 'Collect no more than the amount prescribed for you.'" For most, restitution was virtually impossible—unless one had kept as sharp a tally of his victims as of his justified collections. Accepting forgiveness and resolving to change had to be enough for them.

   ~ *Arrogance.* However, Jesus clearly intended a contrast. The Pharisee's prayer is self-referential, but so again is Mary's Magnificat (Lk 1:46–55):

My soul magnifies the Lord,
and my spirit rejoices in God my Sav-
        ior,
for he has looked with favor
on the lowliness of his servant.
Surely, from now on
all generations will call me blessed;
for the Mighty One has done great
        things for me,
and holy is his name.

The difference is that Mary declares clearly she had done nothing to *deserve* God's favor. That's what grace means.

Hezekiah the Pharisee is elitist ("not like other people"), and lays out his claims to rectitude and scorns those who "don't have the guts to go for the glory." His tithes are not a gift but a concession. He seems to have no need to grow, to change. He's complacent. He's "arrived."

What does the Pharisee miss? The love. He gave tithes to fulfill the Law, not to help the poor. He could be the wedding guest incorrectly dressed or the elder brother in his disdain for the tax collector. There is no righteousness without compassion. At the last judgment (Mt 25), Jesus says the only criterion is *kindness*.

Good to remember that it would be just as self-deceptive to pray, "Thank God, I'm not like this Pharisee."

〜 *Humility*. It's helpful—and certainly spiritually healthy—to remember that the root meaning of *humility* (and *human* and *humor*) is the Latin *humus*, which means "dirt," the lowly substance into which God breathed his Spirit and made Adam, "the man."

Yet another handy oversimplification is to limit that root meaning to "filth." Unfair. It's also the miraculous substance that offers us the food that keeps us alive. A far better understanding is "down to earth"—open eyed, honest.

〜 *Arrogant humility*. Another ironic effect is diametrically opposite to pride: reluctance or fear or even refusal to admit one's virtues. Just as fear of guilt trips points inevitably to narcissistic self-satisfaction, the fear of complacency can corrode into groundless self-hatred. Some of the greatest saints, like Ignatius Loyola, took a long time to realize unbalanced virtue can be evil.

Finally, we serve a God not easily fooled.

12.

The Patient Farmer
MATTHEW 13:3–23; MARK 4:1–20; LUKE 8:5–15

*O*nce upon a time, when everything seemed simpler, in late October when the first rains had softened the ground, a farmer named Benjamin set out to sow his small patch with winter barley. It was resilient grain that stood up to dry weather, even drought—even though its toughness spread to the bread. And for six hundred years, since the Exile, some barley could always be spared to make beer. Benjamin's plot was hedged with nettle bushes from his neighbors' plots and from the path worn hard by heedless passersby hurrying to town through the fields.

From the apron on his belly he plucked handfuls of barley and flung them as carefully as he could from side to side. He tried to keep the precious seed inside the boundaries, but—since Adam—no farmer has been perfect. Some seed flew over the briar bushes onto the road. Some managed to fall through the tough nettles to the ground, and some landed on the small pile of rocks he'd unearthed when he'd plowed last year. Then he fetched his rented bullock and plowed the seed into the shallow earth. When he'd finished the easy part, he went back to his small house for the hard part: waiting.

He busied himself finishing up the summer chores—repairing harness, braiding rope, keeping his children distracted, obeying his wife. Some time each week he went back to the small field, trying to keep ahead of the weeds and birds, but there was no profit in trying to hurry along God's patient work.

As the days passed and the seed worked its slow magic, he saw the small patches where seed had hit the path. It had no chance, what with the birds exercising their own God-given rights. The bit that had fallen in and around the rock pile hardly had a better chance. What had been swept under the bushes found good soil but previous tenants. It sprang up quickly only to be choked. If he had plucked out the weeds, he'd have plucked out whatever barley could have been saved. But he realized—from long practice—that giving in to frustration would be as wasted as the poorly scattered seed.

By far the more important thing was the *field*! The good ground! Within weeks it had brimmed green beyond his wildest hopes, the supple bearded stalks slowly fattening into pods that kept emerging more and more day by day. And as spring began to enliven the hills all round, his crop quickly aged and dried, readying itself for harvest.

And such a harvest! In lucky years his seed multiplied itself tenfold. But this time! A hundredfold would have been impossible. And yet. . . . It was as good as that! And better!

Thoughts to Ponder

~ *Acceptance.* The focus is not on the sower—or even on the seed—but on the receptivity of the audience—which so many liturgists and homilists ignore.

Faith may be a gift of grace, but it has to be *accepted*. And with inescapable logic it follows that those listening have to find the message life-giving and therefore desirable.

I waffled on whether to include this terrific parable simply because my research couldn't resolve a dispute among the biblical experts about *how* the sowing was done. Whereas modern farmers and gardeners spend a lot of time and energy preparing the soil for planting, first-century Palestinian farmers apparently scattered seed and *then* plowed the ground, sometimes hitting hard-packed paths, stone-riddled dirt, and dormant thorns. Which seemed remarkably dumb.

And yet my lifelong experience testified that those in charge of the liturgy, homiletic training, and religious education have been doing precisely that: casting the seed *without* first plowing, without removing the obstacles within the potential converts. The *Universal Catechism* presumes acceptance of the gospel (evangelization) has already occurred. Those directing evangelization want indoctrination rather than conversion, thorough coverage rather than heart-to-heart engagement. They have no tolerance for ambiguity or doubt, no sense (or concern) for receptivities, no willingness to settle for high probability in faith and morals lest they jeopardize comforting certitude. They want catechesis without conversion—or even apologetics.

The root of the word *religion,* however, is *religare,* "to bind fast"; thus, if there's no person-to-Person connection with God, there's no religion. Voltaire knew a great deal more *about* God than Joan of Arc did.

∾ *Self-disrespect.* For the greater part of my lifetime I unerringly identified with all three inhospitable seed receptors. The fact that after decades

and decades, despite my flaws and failures, I was still
here mattered little! I worshiped, confessed, struggled
against my imperfections. But the way my generation
was catechized—motivated by the basest of good mo-
tives (fear and hope of reward)—urged good-hearted
souls to identify with all *but* the good ground. Tragi-
cally poor pedagogy.

   ∽ *Seed is the word of God.* What does that
mean? Not just what's in the Bible. We can't forget
"In the beginning was the Word." God's very first
external self-expression (that we're aware of) was the
universe. As with understanding any other artist, we
can discover so much about our Creator from God's
work. God is unarguably "into" purposeful order:
the predictability of the cosmos, evolution, gradual
personal human development. But the Creator scorns
stasis, business as usual. God's creativity most definitely did *not* stop with the Big Bang. The inescapable
divine plan hinges on death and resurrection; note
that 99 percent of all species God created no longer
exist. Nothing of perishable matter is wasted; everything is recycled, even entire supernovas. God invites
exploration but *never* conquest. Order, yes, but always
surprise. Every Antarctic snowflake is exactly the same
pattern—but each one is unique.

   The Bible is a marvelous book, but it's not the *only*
book. Every other book opens a singular insight into
God—even atheists' books that describe a barren reality bereft of God.

   ∽ *Lost seed.* There is no justification to say
three-quarters of the seed is ultimately wasted. Some
surely is, but only God has a privileged viewpoint to
say which part. Note the huge contrast between the

lost seed and the opulent harvest. About 7 percent was average. A hundredfold was winning the lottery. Hyperbole is a staple of both Old and New Testaments, reemphasizing just what God can do with almost nothing.

◞ *Allegory*. The three Synoptic Gospels follow the parable itself with a point-for-point analysis attributed to Jesus, treating it like an allegory. Stony places are people easily distracted (by "Satan"); "rocky patches" are shallow, enthusiastic for a while, then "I don't get anything out of it." Seeds fallen among "thorns" listen awhile but are finally choked by wealth, discouraged by the cost—surrendering excess, persecutors, or merely dissuaded by sneerers who embarrass us and led to us turning away.

Nearly all experts question whether such commentary comes originally from Jesus. More likely these commentaries are interpretations read into a new situation by the early community. One of the reasons Jesus offers truths in the form of stories is to intrigue listeners to discover the pertinence of the message for themselves—which is the only way truly to assimilate *any* learning.

Nor should the influence of later concerns on the earliest post-Jesus interpretation be any threat to authenticity. For instance, it is hardly likely that when he suddenly grasped the resurrection truth, Doubting Thomas gasped, "My lord and my *God*" (Jn 20:28). He was an inflexible monotheist. It would take centuries before the church had any grasp on such a complex insight. However, just because Thomas didn't actually say those words in the first century doesn't deny they have been true since before the Big Bang. Every word of all four Gospels passed through many hands and minds before settling into its present written form. In fact, the official church has been finding newer insights for more than two thousand years.

Ponder this. A smart young woman in a college theology class challenged me: "Are you trying to make us believe that the atomic theory was true even in the *Middle Ages*?" What was lacking in her perspective? In her humility?

∽ *Who is the sower*? The story doesn't limit the sower to Jesus. He could be any apostolic Christian. Brian Christopher, SJ, suggests the story intends to bolster resolve when the work of evangelizing seems frustrated. It could suggest the same temptation Jesus felt when he wept over Jerusalem. Anyone who has attempted to teach even a single religion class has felt that same unbalanced futility.

Therefore, the message of the parable can be encouraging to any parent or teacher: No matter how tired your arms get from plowing and weeding, it's not all wasted.

∽ *The three obstacles*. The parables were intended initially by Jesus for his own hands-on listeners in early first-century Palestine. The earliest churches tried to apply them meaningfully to their own explicit problems. Presumably, parables were meant to continue to provoke new insights in evolving times. Ignoring for the moment the suspect allegorizing in the Gospels themselves, what are some insights for our same-yet-unique times? What is, first, the well-trodden path and birds; second, rocky soil with no depth; and third, overpowering thorns fighting for their own sustenance and survival?

The surface of the *path* was hard packed, nearly impenetrable. Jesus could have had in mind the Temple elders and their inflexible traditions. But the symbol applies to any teflon-coated attitudes, say, defenses against people of other traditions, races, ethnic origins who are "dangerous." Also, smart, ambitious young women, unathletic boys, overweight girls, gays. Today, religious educators face young people for whom high-school science teachers are as unquestionable as tribal witch doctors used to be. In our own church, theory and historical liturgical practices (and Latin) have become unyielding despite the spiritual needs of the people. The critical—and likely detestable—question here is: Has it ever occurred to us that we might be wrong?

A great deal of Palestinian farmland is little more than two or three inches of topsoil over limestone *bedrock*, not as resistant as the path but shallow, superficial. It would be difficult to find two words more apt than *shallow* and *superficial* for our culture of sound bites, couch potatoes, hook ups that pass for personal connections, complexions/hair/pectorals/abs. How do we evolve and defend deep-rooted convictions in an ethos in which instant gratification takes too long? How do we urge spoiled kids to be "overflowing with thankfulness" (Col 2:7–8)?

Such adolescents and adults might well have a spirituality/religion that is really only what a national spiritual survey calls "moralistic therapeutic deism." Such an unexamined and superficial "belief" allows that some Cosmic Force (cf. "Star Wars") set up a system to provide personal peace and prosperity for *nice* people. "It" doesn't seem interested in much else beyond what our forbears considered good manners. All in all, sort of like Walt Disney. But then, nudged from the pampered nest, they encounter a harsher reality: "I was fine with God, but then my brother died. . . . My Mom became an alcoholic. . . . My Dad left us." They rarely are seduced by wickedness, just disappointment with adult life as it's delivered—like any number or talented, rich, and famous suicides.

These shallow souls are not necessarily self-righteous but supposedly self-sufficient—until reality proves itself intransigent. We have all probably met "self-made men" who might well dive into dangerous waters to save a child but nonetheless complain bitterly about "wetback kids gobbling up my taxes."

Thorns can easily stand for "eminent domain"; "we were here first," "we've *always* done it this way." These souls were the same in Jesus's time. Imagine board rooms today displaying clips from the Sermon on the Mount:

> Do not store up for yourselves treasures on earth, where moth and rust consume and where thieves break in and steal.
>
> You cannot serve God and wealth.
>
> Do not worry about your life, what you will eat or what you will drink, or about your body, what you will wear.
>
> So do not worry about tomorrow; tomorrow will bring worries of its own. Today's trouble is enough for today. (Mt 6)

There is nothing inherently wrong with any of those things. But they are *things* that can take on a life and dominance of their own: idols, false gods. They are fine servants, wicked masters.

They used to call alcohol demon rum. Alcohol isn't a demon, only *our* allowing alcohol to dominate us is a demon. Sex isn't a vice, only the way *we* allow our hormones to manipulate us is a vice. We don't need a devil to explain our antihuman behavior. All God had to do was give freedom to an insufficiently evolved tribe of "apes," and evil was inevitable. Evil means handing over responsibility for your soul to any authority other than the Truth.

Good ground reveals its collaboration in its results:

> The fruit of the Spirit is love, joy, peace, patience, kindness, goodness, faithfulness, gentleness and self-control. Against such things there is no law. Those who belong to Christ Jesus have crucified the sinful nature with its passions and desires. Since we live by the Spirit, let us keep in step with the Spirit. Let us not become conceited, provoking and envying each other. (Gal 5:22–24)

All those heartwarming virtues—"love, joy, peace . . ."—do not fare well in the marketplace either. Nor will our young pick them up from hours of carnage-laden video games. "Do unto others before they do unto you. . . . Never give a sucker an even break. . . . Nice guys finish last. . . . Go for their weak spots." Those convictions are more deeply ingrained in both adults and children than "I have come not to be served but to serve."

If you had a choice of spending a weekend with Jesus or Brad and Angelina . . . ?

Part II

~

Parables in Action

Jesus did not confine himself to spoken parables, but also performed parabolic actions. His most significant parabolic action was his extension of hospitality to the outcasts and their reception into his house, and even into the circle of his disciples. These feasts for publicans are prophetic signs, more significant than words, silent proclamation that the Messianic Age is here, the Age of forgiveness. . . . Jesus not only utters the message of the Kingdom of God; he himself is the message.

—JEREMIAS, *REDISCOVERING*, 179–80

Preach the gospel at all times. If necessary, use words.

—ATTRIBUTED TO ST. FRANCIS OF ASSISI

13.

The Ideal
MARK 10:13–15

*I*t was nearly noon on a market day, and Jesus and his men stopped in a small village by the lake as they trekked from Capernaum to Genesereth to speak in one more synagogue. Judas and Nathaniel went off to the market for food, and the others spread themselves under the trees at the edge of the water.

As they lounged and dozed, a young woman came with a towel over her shoulder, a foot basin on one hip, and her infant slung on the other. She filled the basin with water from the lake and set it to warm in a patch of noon sunlight, preparing to bathe her baby.

She tested the water with her elbow, then set the naked infant in the warm water, and the little boy giggled. He slapped the surface and saw it jump, and he thought so well of himself he did it again. The men who were awake smiled, and Jesus asked the mother, "May I dry him?"

The young woman hesitated. Men didn't do such things. Much less a stranger. But there were plenty of people around, and he looked big and gentle, with an easy grin. So she lifted the infant with the towel and handed him to the smiling young man.

Jesus stroked the silky skin with the rough cloth, careful not to abrade him with his calloused hands, handling the baby as carefully as a spider web. "Ah," he said, and laid the child's head against his own shoulder, the tiny body cradled in the curve of his arm. "Beautiful," he said. He brushed his dark beard against the boy's belly, and both of them giggled.

Just then, a stream of urine arced into the air over Jesus's knees onto the gravel. They all laughed, and Jesus chuckled, "And cheeky!"

Jesus held the naked baby at arm's length over his head. The infant looked down at him, and Jesus stared up at him, both gleeful. "Ah!" Jesus sighed to the little boy, "you are what the kingdom is all about. Guileless and guiltless. Trusting. Unafraid. Untroubled. Unashamed. At such peace!"

The young carpenter's face turned suddenly serious. "If only the others could regain what you have and they've lost. Your mama and papa, your relatives, the people in your village, the priests blinded by their learning."

He held the boy up again at arm's length, and they both giggled. "But some will," Jesus said. "Some will have faith enough to become trusting again."

As they lay dozing, his Twelve hadn't the slightest idea what he meant.

Thoughts to Ponder

 Brevity. This story is brief; it appears in only three verses of Mark's Gospel and four in Matthew (18:1–4), when Jesus answers the disciples' question of who is the greatest in the kingdom by holding up a child. However, it calls for greater attention because of the more intriguing treatment of the same idea in John's Gospel (3:1–21), when the learned and influential council member Nicodemus comes in secret because of his fascination with the message of this young preacher. To the man's dismay, Jesus says no one can enter the kingdom—find enlightenment, fulfillment, ultimate meaning, success in the eyes of God—without being reborn. Taking Jesus literally, the learned man balks at the idea of returning to his mother's womb. As a Pharisee, Nicodemus believed all Jews who kept God's Law would automatically be saved. But, of course, Jesus means a *reorientation*—a conversion, metanoia, transformation of priorities—so radical that it is a rock-bottom restart. "Unless one is born of water and the Spirit, you cannot enter the kingdom of God."

This is a rebirth not of the body but of the soul—a reorientation from most of what we've ingested from the materialist media, the self-indulgent pop culture, placebo religion, parents and peers who love us and want the best for us but have absorbed the same ambient deceptions of our intrusive culture: slovenly thinking, herd need, trivialization of honor, sex, death, the cult of youth, the protraction of adolescence. Who among us can see even the *need* for something better than pampered survival? Such stupor requires a dramatic reversal rarely proposed either to the skeptical young or to their conditioned elders. One suspects the radical invitation Jesus offers would scare too many away.

∿ *Realism*. Obviously, I've taken more liberties than usual with Mark's scene, focusing on a single child rather than the swarms of kids parents were forcing on Jesus—to the disciples' annoyance. And the little boy's innocent stream seemed extraordinarily "fitting." First, it underlines the truth of the incarnation, infusion of divinity into the concrete everyday human.

My temptation was to think that in learning to keep our bodies in check we sadly learned how to keep our souls in check, too—others' expectations, what's "acceptable," what "really matters."

    ❧ *Incarnation.* When God decided to show us what God intended all along for humans to be, the Son accepted *all* that being human entails—not excluding bodily needs and urges theologians tend to pass over in silence. For instance, in order to be fully human (as all Christians profess that he was), Jesus had to doubt, since we are the only species that has that burden. Therefore, Jesus had to live *without* the assurance of the divine knowledge—which would preclude even hesitation. As Paul says, "He *emptied* himself, taking the form of a slave." To put it perhaps too crudely, he freely chose to become "amnesiac" about what God knows. Similarly, because of waves of doctrinal disputes about the values of the flesh (even though God himself found it desirable), touch seems to many to be dangerous, an occasion of sin, a slippery slope—thus unwarily insulting the God who invented it and "saw it was good."

    Jesus had carpenter's hands. He didn't hesitate to touch a leper. He cured a blind man by touching his eyes with mud and spit. He opened a man's deaf ears with his fingertips, offered his scars to Thomas's probing fingers. At his arrest he picked up the ear of the servant Peter had so impetuously struck off and healed the man. Every sacrament hinges on touch. Perhaps this is one more place we can stop imposing our limitations on God.

    ❧ *The faith of children.* Like the chicken/egg claim to priority, the conflict between "childish" and "childlike" is age old. What did Jesus ask for when he placed one of very few obstacles to a kingdom ready to accept whores and con artists before self-righteous puritans? What do children have that nearly all adults surrender to sophistication, skepticism, profit motives, self-interest?

"And a little child shall lead them" (Is 11:6). Children are unafraid of being embarrassed or awed. They never weary but are often wearying in their curiosity (that's stifled by second grade). They think with their hearts, like Simon Peter. They accept dependency. Ideally, they have an unshakable core conviction that they *belong*. They're intuitive, imaginative. They're extremely aware and frighteningly unwary. Their world's suffused with enchantment, wonder, curiosity. They stand open mouthed in front of a swaybacked old horse. With an empty carton and crayons they can create a whole universe. As God did. Not from need; just for the sheer fun of it. Look at the wonders the childlike Spielberg spins out of his imagination. Einstein, a true child-man, said, "Imagination is more important than knowledge." But tell that to the experts who control the SATs, the curricula, the texts.

Genuine faith is a rebirth—in adulthood—of a totally "new" self/soul/person, one with an intensely richer perspective, grasping a new "way of looking at things." Those warped in adolescence by a "need" for sophistication and materialist demands expunge from their values anything that smacks of "softness," which effectively bars any hope for Christianity. The poet William Blake captured that empowering childhood with skill:

> To see a World in a Grain of Sand
> And a Heaven in a Wild Flower,

> Hold Infinity in the palm of your
>   hand
> And Eternity in an hour.

Churchill said, "My education was interrupted only by my schooling." Many don't get an education at all, just a diploma certifying they haven't been too troublesome.

"You've gotta keep your guard up, gang. Everybody's out to take you. They're feeling out the weakness in your defenses. Never talk to strangers. Real men never cry. It's a jungle out there." And it *is* a jungle out there. You wanna know why? Precisely because of all that defensive satanic advice. Analysis, decisiveness, clarity are essential human values. But without the balance of their opposites they cease to be good servants and become domineering masters.

     ∽ *Lopsided values.* If the pervasive subservience to pragmatism and profit begin early to unbalance our children's openness to the will of God—manifest in their natures and in the call of Christ—what concrete and specific ways can we challenge that, curtail it, convince our young to *internalize* the desire to be better than other animals, to aspire even beyond fulfilled humanity?

Don't for a moment think that's easy. The media control them more hours every single day than we do. And the media manipulators are professionals, slick, seductive. They appeal to the least common denominator, what Freudians call the Id, the beast within us from whom we are invited to evolve.

"My kids used to be so enthusiastic, so creative, when they were younger!"

So were you.

What would happen if some emissary from Middle Earth or Hogwarts cast a spell that sucked out the energy from all the batteries on earth? Neutralized every outlet of the Electronic Matrix that has eroded the need for children to develop imagination, from cave fires to the old Sonora radio luring kids on a journey with Jack Armstrong and Betty Fairchild up the Amazon?

Walks in the woods—with iPods and smartphones left home? More time with empty boxes and Magic Markers? A school play, even if it means a season without a sport? Art/music electives instead of one more math class to outwit the draconian SAT? Frustration over their desensitizing will do nothing. Hope is never near enough.

    ~ *Magic.* What we have lost is susceptibility to enchantment. Einstein kept it. So did his predecessors, the Magi, foolish enough to risk their fortunes, their lives—and their reputations! To follow a star. And then, the simplicity that once enabled learned kings from the East to see God hidden within an infant lying in a manger.

14.

Benefits Forgotten
LUKE 17:11–15

*J*esus and his followers began their journey south to Jerusalem, through Samaria. Because of the ethnic antagonism, it was not the safest route, but the other road along the far side of Jordan was twenty miles longer, hotter, and a steeper climb through a desolate wasteland of barren rock with twisted canyons and cliffs.

It was a foolhardy journey from the start. Even the gullible ones knew the powers in the city would no longer tolerate Jesus. It would take all his uncanny powers to keep them all from prison. If not far worse. But Jesus had set his face inflexibly toward his destiny.

Late one afternoon early in the journey they were trudging toward the Wadi Bathshean on the ill-defined border between Galilee and Samaria. Up ahead, between them and the town a half mile or so away, they saw a cluster of hooded figures. No way of telling men from women. As they got closer, they slowed. The strangers had no staves or weapons showing. Perhaps they were sick and had heard rumors the healer was coming. Or maybe they were begging. Or highwaymen. There were ten of them.

One of them brought his cupped hands out of his sleeves to his mouth, and the disciples saw. He had only stubs of scabby fingers, only two holes where a man's nose should be. They caught glimpses of the other hideous faces shadowed in their cowls, skin deeply cracked like dried-up stream beds, covered in tuberous red and bleached patches. Faces from a nightmare, suspended above bodies like rags draped over sticks.

Worse than armed bandits. Lepers! Driven from their lifelong family homes and towns. Forced to shout or ring bells to keep their contagion from the fortunate. A few had relatives who left food for them near the graveyards where they gathered so as not to be utterly alone. Most had no one else. They were not just ritually unclean but monstrous and, so it was believed, savagely contagious. They weren't allowed close enough to beg. Their only hope was garbage.

The man's lungs wheezed as he tried to shout. "Jesus! Master!" he cried. "*Mercy?*"

Jesus's followers looked sharply at him. Once before, near the lake, he'd actually touched one of them, and his Twelve had given the master a wide berth for weeks after. But this time he was strangely reserved.

Jesus raised his hand, looking for a moment back at his own terrified men, then spoke to the lepers. "Go quickly to the priest's house in the village. Have him testify you are clean."

The ten lepers pulled their ghastly hands from their armpits and examined them. They were still ragged and pustulant. Was this really the healer they'd heard was on his way?

"But . . . ," the first one who had spoken rasped, "we are not allowed into a town."

Jesus turned to John, the swiftest. "Run to the gate. Tell the keeper to summon the priest. Have him bring what he needs to declare a leper clean."

Obediently, skirting the lepers, John set off at a long-limbed lope the half-mile to the village. Jesus said to the lepers. "It's all right. Go now. Meet the priest by the entry."

Dumbly, the lepers turned toward the town and began to hobble back along the stony road. The Twelve watched them, hunched and limping along, bewildered.

Suddenly from the pack of moving rags, they heard a terrifying scream!

"*Whole*!" came the raw voice. "My hand is *whole* again! My arm is *whole* again!"

In an instant, all the lepers were screaming, too, laughing and shoving one another. The voices drifted back to the Twelve. "I can *feel* my feet! . . . Smooth! Like a child's! . . . My face!"

Sooner than they expected, the flustered village priest appeared with a group of curious villagers at the head of the street into the village. He listened to the jabbering a moment, checked their faces and outstretched hands none too carefully. Obviously he now faced a ritual few priests ever found need for, and he began to improvise some sort of rite from his recollections of the holy books. He remembered something about scarlet yarn and a branch of hyssop and two birds, one to be slain and the other freed. But there was only his son's pigeon, which he dared not kill. The boy stood at the priest's side with a basin of water red with chicken blood, carrying his pigeon.

The priest took the skittery bird and dipped its grey breast into the bloody basin, then hurled it free into the air. It circled overhead, then headed back over the clay roofs. The disciples were now close enough to hear him nervously improvising as he dipped the sprig of hyssop into the bloody water and sprinkled the cured lepers. "Now, uh, to the synagogue, to burn your clothes and to, uh, the *mikveh* to bathe and be welcomed back into the people."

So the ten men and women Jesus had cured fairly danced behind the priest, freed from a life of despair, into a town for the first time in years, eager to be on their way back to spouses and children they had been forbidden for so long to touch or even to come too near.

That warm night, not wishing a confrontation with the locals and because they were too poor for an inn, Jesus and his men slept beneath the trees outside the town. Next morning, they woke and stretched, sat slowly up, scratching sand from the corners of their eyes.

And there he stood. Waiting. For Jesus. The man who had first spoken for the others.

He was perhaps forty years old, but now with smooth skin burnished by the sun, his head ritually shaven, clad in someone's castoffs. He waited patiently until Jesus raised himself up and stood. Then he ran full tilt up to Jesus and threw himself at his feet, kissing them, and murmuring, "Thank you, Master," and "Praise the God of all mercies!"

Jesus helped him to his feet and reached his thumbs up to wipe the man's tears. "Peace, my brother," Jesus said. "Now, quickly . . . home! Your faith has saved you."

And the man turned and ran quickly down the highway, whooping with delight.

Two of the Twelve rose and walked into the town to buy some breakfast. Jesus turned to the others and sat down with them, ready for the morning prayers.

"Odd, isn't it," Jesus said. "Not odd, I suppose. More like the usual thing. There were ten of them, yes? Yet only one felt the need to thank God."

Each man covered his eyes with his right hand and breathed: "*Sh'ma Yisraeil, Adonai Eloheinu, Adonai Echad.* . . . Hear, O Israel, the Lord is our God, the Lord is One."

Thoughts to Ponder

∾ *Despair*. It's enlightening to consider what kept these men and women from despair before Jesus came into their lives. Also, to wonder how many of the people we encounter every day are clinging onto some frail reason to keep going.

∾ *Jesus's attitude*. A sensitive eye and ear catches an uncharacteristic brusqueness in Jesus in this encounter. He "keeps his distance." There is no direct contact. As Luke often does in his telling, I tried to suggest it might have been his concern for the wavering faith of his own men. Perhaps, too, it could have been a further challenge to the victims' faith—though such upping the ante seems *too* untypical. However, this miracle is like Elisha's telling the hesitant pagan leper Naaman to go wash himself seven times in the Jordan (2 Kgs 5:10–15).

∾ *Faith*. The cure was possible not as a result of *obedience*—as some commentators insist—but as simple trust in Jesus. Nowhere is there an indication before the miracle that the lepers believe Jesus is a conduit of *divine* power. Only that he is some kind of healer. The grateful leper's conjunction of thanks to Jesus *and* to God is a leap upward. And yet all ten did rise to the faith challenge Jesus imposed on them to turn around (a genuine symbol) and trust his implied promise that they would indeed be cured before they reached the priest. Then it could happen.

Nowhere does Jesus ever perform a miracle to provoke faith, only in response to it.

   ∾ *Contagion.* We now know that leprosy (Hansen's Disease) is not as fearsomely contagious as simpler cultures believed. Leprosy is probably less contagious than the flu. You really have to live for some years in an epidemic area to risk catching it, and antibiotics now eliminate it in a few months. Nonetheless, given what everyone in the parable believed true, the story underlines yet again Jesus's utter lack of fastidiousness in those he welcomes—not merely the ritually unclean (like politicians who vote "wrongly" or people in "unlawful" marriages) but the utterly repulsive and genuinely contagious. Some otherwise admirable Christians find it impossible to find much compassion for victims of AIDS.

   ∾ *"We Lepers."* Perhaps the most famous leper in history is the heroic Belgian priest Damien de Voester, SSCC, who volunteered in 1873 to minister to the eight hundred lepers marooned for the safety of others on the Hawaiian island of Molokai. They lived in unspeakable squalor, but despite opposition from every side, Damien took the situation in hand. He imposed discipline and sanitation; dressed their wounds; enlisted volunteers to build houses, roads, a reservoir; began working farms; and built a school for infected children.

He was canonized in 1995. The book *Damien the Leper* by John Farrow is available, as well as a film, "Molokai," and a DVD titled "An Uncommon Kindness," narrated by Robin Williams. Of special interest is the brilliant defense of Damien by Robert Louis

Stevenson against insulting charges laid against him by Pastor C. M. Hyde, who publicly vilified Damien as "coarse" and "careless."

With a matador's skill Stevenson wrote to Hyde:

> You are one of those who have an eye for faults and failures; that you take a pleasure to find and publish them; and that, having found them, you make haste to forget the overvailing virtues and the real success which had alone introduced them to your knowledge. It is a dangerous frame of mind.

But the point of mentioning Damien is that, after ten tireless years, he accidentally scalded himself one day with boiling water. But he felt nothing. At his next mass he began his homily: "*We* lepers." It is a humble declaration with which we can all unite.

       Ingratitude. This is one more place in the Gospel that gives aid and comfort to our internal enemies who find willful wickedness where there is merely self-centered thoughtlessness. These cured lepers were so drunk with joy that all they could think of was the people they loved—which is hardly reprehensible in itself. It's remotely like a jubilant Olympic medalist running first to the arms of her parents or boyfriend rather than to her coach.

And all ten did do everything that Jesus asked them to. In that, they're not unlike the elder brother of the prodigal son. Dutiful. Even though they missed the main point.

Nonetheless, few of us are not culpable of what Shakespeare called "benefits forgot," casually taking for granted what are so close to miracles, like stupefying sunsets and summer skies crowded with stars, an infant's whole fist encircling an adult's pinkie finger, hearing "I love you, too." Such moments led e. e. cummings to write:

> how should tasting touching hearing
>   seeing
> breathing any—lifted from the no
> of all nothing—human merely being
> doubt unimaginable You?

Each of us is so staggeringly gifted, it's a wonder even the least sensitive could hold themselves from rushing to the feet of our Creator in stunned gratitude. Chesterton writes:

> Children are grateful when Santa Claus puts in their stockings gifts of toys or sweets. Could I not be grateful to Santa Claus when he put in my stockings the gift of two miraculous legs?

That is the reason *Eucharist* means "thanksgiving."

The agents of our benefactions are uncountable. I know I never got around to telling my parents, "Thank you for taking the risk of having me." I did get a chance to thank the nun who gave me a passion for reading, but I never thanked the crusty old Jesuit who taught me to write concretely with my first concern for the audience. Nor the other Jesuit who gave me the part of Cassius in "Julius Caesar" when I was resigned to carrying a spear.

I sometimes have been almost literally "struck" by grace when I'm wallowing in self-pity. The Spirit goes "psst!" in my innermost ear and says, "Take a piece of paper and start to write the names of everybody you love and who loves you." Even such a cozy, cuddly enemy as self-pity just can't stand up to that over-whelming truth.

          ∾ *Delight*. We have the option, if we choose to take it, to be grateful for the undeserved gift of existence—and all the gifts that follow from that one. Everything—absolutely everything—becomes incomparably precious and thrilling when we grasp the truth that we might never have had it. When Robinson Crusoe was marooned on his deserted island, every bit of debris he found from the shipwreck was a treasure.

    Gratitude makes us better people.

15.

One Plucky Lady
JOHN 4:4–26

*O*nce upon a time Jesus and the Twelve were passing through unfriendly Samaria on their way home from Jerusalem, and they came to a famous spot called Jacob's Well, just outside a large town called Sychar. Looming beyond the town was Mount Gerizim, sacred to Samaritans, who believe it the place Yahweh preferred his true temple to be. On the right of the road, where it bends from the plain of Makhneh into the pass of Shechem, sat the holy well dug by the patriarch Jacob, the first piece purchased by a Hebrew in the promised land. Jacob bequeathed the small plot to his son, Joseph, the one sold into slavery by his jealous brothers and, by God's grace, elevated to vizier of the pharaoh and savior of the Hebrews from famine. In the Exodus, the story goes, Moses took Joseph's bones with him and buried them within a few feet of his father's well.

The land was hardscrabble, dusty, and scrubby. Every scuff raised dust devils into the hot air. It was near noon, so the Twelve dispersed into the village to find affordable provisions and left Jesus sitting on the circular lip of the well, under a solitary tree shading one side.

Shimmering in the heat haze along the pebbly road from the town came the figure of a woman with a clay jar on each shoulder. She appeared to be at least forty, full figured, and tinkling with bells on her wrists and dangling earrings. Her brows were dark and heavy, set in a fixed scowl above her large dark eyes.

When she caught sight of Jesus, she hesitated. Her eyes flashed in their shadows. Difficult to tell if it was merely a twinkle or a glint of steel. Most likely both. Her whole demeanor said she tolerated neither fools nor philanderers. But for some reason she was coming to the town well at the hottest time of the day, long after most village women had drawn their day's water. And she had no daughters to do it for her.

"Shalom," Jesus said.

She said nothing, pretending to ignore him, but Jesus waited for her.

"Your accent's Galilean," she finally said. "You are a '*true*' Jew?" she asked, not looking directly at him.

"I think I am."

"And you speak to me? A woman? And a Samaritan dog?"

"Samaritan, true. Surely not a dog."

"Mongrel, then."

"Only different from me."

"You're not as finicky as your fellows."

"That is also quite true."

She fixed the handle of one of her jars to the hook on the well rope and began to lower it.

He smiled. "May I have a drink from your jar?"

The weathered woman looked puzzled. She hesitated with her jar dripping on the rim.

Jesus said, "If you could only see the gift God offers you at this moment, and who it is offering the gift, you would be asking *me* for water. Living water."

"'Living water?' Running water. Out here in the dust and scrub?"

"No. Water brimming with life."

"Sir, you have nothing to draw with, and this well is very, very deep."

"You have a jar full of water." He cupped his hands. "And I brought my own cup."

She chuckled and poured some cold water into his hands. "With your living water, you're not greater than Jacob, are you? He dug this well himself. His sons and flocks drank from it. So have we. For centuries. This living water of yours is better than ours?"

Jesus tipped his cupped hands to his face and drank. He brushed them against his tunic and nodded his thanks. Then he said, "Anyone who drinks the water from your well will become thirsty again, yes? But whoever drinks the water I offer will never be thirsty again. Not ever."

She cocked an eye at him and brought her fist to her chin.

He nodded once and he went on. "Water that breeds eternal life, gushing up to become an unfailing spring of aliveness within your soul."

She lifted her other water jar from the ground to the edge of the well, for something to do.

"Everlasting life," he said.

She was silent a long while, and then she whispered fervently. "Sir, give me this water. So I may never be thirsty or need to come back to this well again."

Jesus took a breath. "Go call your husband."

She scowled. Then she said, almost inaudibly, "I . . . have no husband."

The smile on Jesus's face broadened. "Ah, *good*! You're absolutely truthful to say you have no husband. You've had five husbands, yes? And the man you're with now isn't really a real husband, is he? Honesty. It's the first step home."

Her eyes grew wide and she sank to sit on the rim of the well, open mouthed.

"How did you . . . ?" But the answer presented itself within her. "Sir," she said, "I . . . I don't understand. But . . . you are . . . a prophet. A completely different . . ."

"Yes."

"Our ancestors, back almost forever, have worshiped at this holy mountain. But you Jews say the only place for true worship is Jerusalem. Must we . . . ?"

Jesus held up his hand gently. "Woman, believe me. We are at the brink of a new time. The moment is coming—no, it's already here—when you'll worship the Father not just on this mountain *or* on Mount Zion. The place is not important anymore. Only who you *truly* are. True worshipers will meet the Father in spirit and in truth, which is where the Father seeks them."

The woman could scarcely breathe. "I know the Messiah is coming, sir. I believe it. And when he comes, he will . . . he will explain . . . well, everything."

Jesus said quietly, "Yes. Here I am."

They sat silently together awhile in the shade of the tree. Then they looked up as they heard voices coming to them along the road from the town. The Twelve. The woman rose, bowed to Jesus, and hurried down the road, forgetting her water jars.

When the Twelve had caught sight of Jesus and the woman sitting on the rim of the well, they'd slowed to a stop. Quizzical. Some scowling. It was very unusual. Improper. As the woman hurried past them, avoiding their eyes, some of them stared at her with equal impropriety.

They came to the well and settled themselves on the ground in the shade, and kept pushing food on Jesus, but he nodded it away, staring after the woman as she made her way quickly into the town.

"I'm not really hungry," he said. When they kept insisting, he said, "I have food you don't know about."

He saw their bewilderment and said, "My food is knowing the work of my Father is beginning. The planting, the slow teasing of the crop. I can feel it. The harvest. I can feel it beginning, surging under my feet!"

When they finished eating their fruit and bread and before they could settle into their afternoon siesta, villagers began to appear along the road. The woman had told them about the prophet, right out there at their own well. She'd spread the word. "He *couldn't* be the real Messiah, could he? But he told me everything I've ever done! He's *some* kind of prophet."

So the whole flock of them—Samaritans!—sat in the blistering heat, listening to this young Jew opening a totally unheard of way of living: how to succeed by yielding. They were so fascinated by him they begged him to stay with them awhile. So he and his men stayed a few days but finally left for the other towns.

Perhaps it wasn't at all odd, but it took a few more days. And it was only one or two of her fellow villagers who managed to tell her, "You were right. Thank you."

Thoughts to Ponder

∽ *A woman.* Some commentators question whether this episode could ever have happened. No woman of that time or place would have had the ability to engage Jesus in serious theological discussion—much less such witty badinage. Women didn't have the intelligence. They were unschooled—as if schooling initiates the capacity to think. Thus, they claim, she was "confused" about this living water Jesus offered. She was no more confused than the carefully selected male apostles were, at every juncture, and no more confused over living water than Nicodemus—the absolute opposite of this outcast untutored female— was about rebirth in the previous chapter. *All* of them were confused because Jesus was introducing them to insights even the great thinkers hadn't yet entertained.

∾ *Impropriety* is too mild a word for this whole scenario. In all scripture this is the longest conversation between Jesus and anyone else, and he seems utterly unconcerned that he was openly *scandalous* on at least four counts: talking to a woman, alone, and a half-breed Samaritan at that, *and* drinking water from an "unclean" jug. No Hebrew man would talk with any woman in the street—not even his own mother, sister, daughter or wife.

Such bravado means little to us, but the reaction of a proper Jew at the time would be not unlike any normal Catholic seeing the front page of a check-out tabloid picturing an archbishop exiting a Las Vegas brothel.

It shows to what lengths the Christian apostle will go—what opprobrium he or she will risk—to rescue a wounded soul. It's a disconcerting habit in Jesus so many overly dedicated Christians ignore: his blithe disregard for differences and for those who think them important.

∾ *Husbands*. When Jesus tells her to go for her husband, we discover this woman has had five husbands (the word choice at least suggests legal marriages) and is now living with a man who is not her "proper" husband. Many commentators have jumped to the conclusion that she was an immoral woman who had been divorced five times, yet the text says nothing of divorce.

A single actual clue is only suggestive and circumstantial: She comes to the well at a very unlikely hour. Critics merely assume this is habitual. And that the motive is to avoid contact with her catty neighbors. Nothing can determine why any one conjecture outweighs another.

These vague hints draw out the very worst in the self-righteous. Pastor John Piper calls her "a worldly, sensually-minded, unspiritual harlot from Samaria" and uses the word "harlot" six more times in the same three-page Internet sermon. A painful number of worthy Christians impose their own judgmentalism on the ever-so-welcoming Jesus. At *no* point does Jesus invite repentance from this woman, nor does he even hint she ought to reconsider her living arrangements, nor, for that matter, does he criticize her or speak of sin at all.

Girls were married at least by fifteen, quite commonly to men ten to twenty years older, when forty was a long life. Therefore, multiple marriages were not uncommon. Since society decreed male-centered households, she would remarry for legal, economic, and social *identity*. This is a major point of the story: on many points she was a non-person. (Wise to recall that despite the evident wisdom of the men who framed the American Constitution, females were not acknowledged as legal "persons" until August 18, 1920, when the nineteenth amendment was ratified.)

Perhaps she was unsatisfyingly sterile. Perhaps this most recent man had grown children from an earlier marriage, and he wanted to control the inheritance. Perhaps it was what's so common today, living together,

which—despite all claims to open-minded sophistication—still raises eyebrows. Undeniably, she had been
passed from hand to hand. Still, there must have been
something intriguing about her beyond being a mere
sexual convenience or an unpaid servant.

    ~ *Confidence*. Despite her many men she
shows that she is her own woman. That's why critics
give this unusual story so much attention. Like Mary
Magdalene, she's one of the few characters in the
Gospels (along with Peter, Judas, and Thomas) who
has a personality. Which could be one of the reasons
her husbands found her desirable. She was interested
in more than household chores. She's there getting the
water. But that's not who she is.

Jesus has seen her, and he's treated her as an *equal*,
engaging in the theological ping-pong that delighted
Hebrew men like Tevye in "Fiddler on the Roof." Like
Jesus, she is an absolutely unacceptable contradiction:
a very bright woman. As the estimable Dr. David Lose
says of her: "Because Jesus has 'seen' her, she sees
herself. He has seen her plight of dependence, not im-
morality." Jesus offers her *dignity*.

Whatever the reasons, Jesus sees she's wounded,
worn out, shamed. He ignores her moral life completely. The woman's moral life may intrigue the punc-
tilious, but it seems of no interest at all to Jesus. He
emphasizes its irrelevance by raising the subject then
dismissing it. He shows that opening her life to eternity
is far more worthy a question than her bedmates.

    ~ *Living water*. In such a parched climate,
water was a critical, precious matter of life and death.
As supernatural life rises above and amplifies ordinary

human life, the life Jesus offers is meant to *exhilarate* human living. Our being Christian should make us recognizably more alive. The seemingly insignificant detail of leaving her water jars behind could reinforce the lesson that she has now concentrated her hopes on a life beyond the need for material sustenance.

၏ *Salvation*. This story isn't about sin. It's about salvation: rescuing a "lost soul." The pivotal question seems to be, Who's got the best salvation? God revealed on Mount Zion or on Mount Gerazim? When the woman asks Jesus about worship, she's not diverting their talk from her shameful marital status; she's using her very good mind to question this prophet on the core issue of the centuries-old feud between Jewish and Samaritan theology.

Jesus solves the dilemma. First, he himself and all he says and does is *the* revelation of what salvation means. He is, in fact, greater than Jacob, but the question of worship—where or better—is no longer a valid question. This water will well up within her. Where we worship God and how we do it seem less important to Jesus than the fact that we do it—sincerely. Those who worship God, worship in spirit and truth. Wherever.

၏ *Conversion*. Genuine conversion requires the slow erosion of inflexible preconceptions. Aristotle said that in the well-made play, the instant of recognition of truth coincides perfectly with the turning point: the spiritual rebirth. When Oedipus finally grasps the truth about who the gods are and who he is in contrast to them, then comes the *metanoia*, conversion.

Like most conversions, hers is not instantaneous. For a long time in their verbal dalliance, she stays on a literal level. At first, this stranger is just a thirsty, pushy Jew. Only slowly does he begin to interest her, then to intrigue her. Then she tests his claim to prophetic insight by deepening the question to authentic worship. Even after she senses he's talking on a more profound level, she clings to her notion of literal water, the kind she might no longer need to labor for. Then intuition clicks in. Commentators note her gradual descriptions of Jesus: "Jew" (9) . . . "Sir" (11) . . . "Prophet" (19) . . . and finally, "Christ" (29). Her recognition of who Jesus truly is was as progressive as it was for the witnesses to the resurrection.

Note, too, that her conversion is brought about not from some profound spiritual insight but is based solely on his detailed knowledge of her marital situation, and she ever so slowly gets to the point where she calls him *the* Messiah. What moves the discussion to a transcendent level is the major shift of the locus of legitimate worship.

Those who claim to evangelize and catechize could well ponder the ways Jesus taught.

~ *Evangelization.* What's the first thing you do when you have great news? Find a lost coin, a lost sheep, a lost son? Get engaged, pregnant, promoted? She left her water jars and ran to spread the good news. What do you do when you encounter your teacher risen from the dead? And her belief became contagious, despite her lack of certitude. St. John Chrysostom writes that this woman immediately believed, showing that she was not only much wiser than Nicodemus but also more courageous.

Also, Jesus here leaves the confines of traditional Judaism and ventures into a reality Jews believed to be a No Man's Land between the truth and despicable paganism. He refuses to be boxed in by human expectations or intolerance.

16.

Negating Death

*W*hen the worst of the spring rains had dwindled, the relatives of Jesus in Galilee began to suggest, with some insistence, that he take his layabouts and traveling circus elsewhere, like maybe Jerusalem, where snake charmers were more or less normal. Which happily coincided with plans Jesus had already made. The more prudent—not to say skittish—of the Twelve suggested, in view of increased pestering from the authorities, *any* other place might be more promising. But Jesus kept insisting on his Father's "plan," as if that explained anything. So Thomas, the faithful skeptic, mumbled, "Hell, if that's the plan, we might just as well go up to the city and die with him." So they set off, this time down the eastern side of the river with a caravan bound for Jerusalem through pagan Perea.

Somewhere along their journey—and God knows how the messenger found them—news came from the family they usually stayed with in Bethany, just outside the city: Martha, the eldest, Mary the youngest, and their brother, Lazarus. It was urgent. Lazarus was dying.

His men knew how beloved Lazarus and his sisters were to Jesus, but he simply nodded, and said, "Yes. We will come. But this illness will not end in death. It's a moment for God's glory to shine." And yet he made no move even to rise from where he sat.

And so it was for two more days, during which Jesus spoke to a few interested pagans a few times a day but made no move at all to go to his friends who were in need.

Finally, on the third morning, he rose and picked up his staff. "All right," he said. "Time enough. Our friend Lazarus is asleep. I'm going to wake him."

One of them, only too aware of what Jerusalem meant to them, said, "Well, if he's only asleep, maybe there's no need to . . . "

Jesus frowned and said, quite decisively, "Lazarus is dead."

Which did he mean?

He went on. "I'm so happy, for your sake, I wasn't there. It will help you believe."

Whatever that meant, it at least didn't seem to make believing easier.

They trekked on down the road to Jericho, then up the torturously steep highway toward Jerusalem, cutting off just before it along the ridge to Bethany, two miles southeast of the city. As the group passed, people recognized Jesus from previous visits, and some told the men he was too late. Lazarus was dead. Four days ago. Word swept ahead of them, so Martha was standing there at the village entry with a few mourners. The custom was to come to the tomb for three days because the dead person's spirit lingered among them and departed only on the fourth day.

Martha stood a little ahead of the others. Her face was ravaged and glistened with tears. But she stood straight, in full possession of herself. She turned to the woman next to her and said, "Fetch Mary." The woman scurried off into the town.

Jesus approached and touched Martha's cheek. She said, stiffly, "Master, if . . . if you had come sooner . . . " She roughly palmed away the tears and composed herself. "But I know that, even now, God's power is with you."

Jesus said softly, "Martha, haven't I helped you see death does not win?"

She interrupted, grim. "Yes. Of course. I know Lazarus will rise." Her mouth pinched. "Eventually. On the last day."

Jesus took both her hands and bent to look into her eyes, but she lowered them, staring hard at the road. "Martha, *I* am the resurrection. The pathway to life. Whoever believes who I am will *never* truly die. Can you believe that?"

She bit her lower lip, and slowly her eyes lifted to meet his. She took a deep breath. "Yes, my Lord. I believe. I believe you are the Messiah. The Son of God. Come among us."

Just then Mary ran out onto the high road and fell at Jesus's feet. He lifted her, and she clung to him, her eyes brimming. Like Martha, she said, "Lord, if only you'd been here."

Behind her came all the people who had been sitting *shiva*, many even from Jerusalem, a few moaning and beating their breasts affectedly.

Jesus looked really annoyed at them. "Where have you laid him?" he asked. So they led him along the road into a grove at the base of a rock face honeycombed with natural niches. Each of those near ground level was blocked by a near-circular flat stone.

Jesus stood silent a moment, praying, tears gathering in his eyes, almost against his will. Some of the onlookers whispered, "See how he loved the man?" Others sniggered, "If he did, what took 'im so long? Ain't he the one makes blind folks see?"

Jesus stood and then spoke grimly. "Roll away the stone."

Martha tugged at his sleeve. "Master, it's four days. The smell."

Jesus looked down at her. "Didn't I tell you? I know it's hard. But believe."

Some men shouldered the stone aside, levering with crooks and staves.

Jesus lowered his eyes, and they could hear him pray. "Father, I know you hear me. Always. Help them believe they needn't fear death ever again." He squared his shoulders and shouted: "Lazarus! Come *out*!"

The Twelve looked at one another, wondering what the Master had set himself to this time. The onlookers stared, held their breath, set their jaws, daring him.

A gray shape materialized in the dark opening. The crowd stood slack-mouthed, paralyzed. The dead man hobbled, ankles constrained by the shroud. His sisters rushed to him and carefully pulled away the gauze napkin from his face.

The young man stood there, blinking, bewildered.

"Unbind him, and set him free," Jesus said.

From the edge of the group of mourners two men slipped quietly away. To bring the story to their masters.

Thoughts to Ponder

༄ *Authenticity*. The first thorny question, of course, is this: Did this actually happen? We could as well ask the same question of all Jesus's miracles.

My too-cavalier response: If you claim to be a Christian—of any tradition—that, ipso facto, declares an acceptance of resurrection. St. Paul put it boldly: "If Christ has not been raised, your faith is futile" (1 Cor 15:17). We simply can't be authentic Christians without accepting the miracle of resurrection.

In order to accept such a reality, it is equally inescapable that there *must* then be a dimension to reality—to our lives and to our importance—that defies the limits of time and space. What we accept of reality firsthand, tangibly and rationally, is thoroughly permeated by another dimension that is *super*-natural: human life but more intensely alive.

There is no way to "prove"—incontestably—that Jesus or Lazarus or anybody else can defy death. No more so than one can "prove"—incontestably—that the Big Bang and all the events and creations embedded in it actually transpired. All such assertions—including every single claim about the progress of evolution—are not based on eyewitness accounts but on reasoned conclusions from solid evidence. The solid evidence for the resurrection of Jesus is the "deathbed confessions" of those who went to excruciating deaths rather than deny their experience of the risen Jesus. If we can yield our doubts about the resurrection of Jesus, then accepting all the other miracles in the Gospels becomes less prickly.

And one might add that, if we even accept that there had to be a Creator to explain the predictability of the universe, we're squarely on the slippery slope to faith. If there is *some* Mind-Behind-It-All who turned nothing into everything—He/She/They (but not It) can do whatever He/She/They please. Open a path in the Red Sea, allow men to walk on water, defy death. We already conceded that He/She/They can do *anything*.

⤳ *Lazarus* appears several times in the Gospels but says not a word. (The fact that no version fabricates some dialogue in which he describes his brief sojourn in the afterlife is actually an argument toward their truthfulness. Why?)

Unlike him—and so many other gospel characters—his sisters have at least rough-sketched personalities. From other passages we can legitimately infer that *Martha* is the "take charge" one who has little patience with her sister mooning at the feet of the teacher while she's out walloping the pots. In their subtle dialogue we can discern that Martha knows her "catechism," but he's calling on her faith—which is quite a different matter. *Mary*, in sharp contrast, is "a young girl." She is the one who, impulsively, broke into a dinner and anointed Jesus from a jar of spikenard perfume. Judas—quite reasonably—was irate at the waste. The perfume was worth a year's wages, thousands of dollars in today's terms, brought at ridiculous effort from the mountains of India. But it exemplifies the indiscriminate response of the true believer.

⤳ *The delay.* Jesus sometimes acts in a manner that twitches simple faith. For instance, he snaps angrily at Peter, calling him "you Satan," when Peter is only trying to save his friend from harm (Mt 16:23); his mother and relatives ask to see him, and he leaves them outside (Mk 3:33); his mother mentions the embarrassing wine situation at Cana, and he says, "Woman, what concern is that to you and to me? My hour has not yet come" (Jn 2:4); he says, "Whoever comes to me and does not hate father and mother, wife and children, brothers and sisters, yes, and even life itself, cannot be my disciple" (Lk 14:26).

His brusqueness gives us pause. *Which is precisely what he intended.* It's overstated for a reason, and Jesus often gives the reason—even though the usual wording is foreign to us, for example, "You are setting your mind not on divine things but on human things" (Mt 16:23). In other words, "You're trying to tell God what he would do if he were as smart as you are."

This apparently consistent response to prayers—even of those undeniably precious to Jesus personally—is difficult to remember when God doesn't answer *our* prayers as efficiently as he cured lepers and cripples. Our Lady knew how to pray. She simply posed a problem Jesus likely already knew about and left it to him to decide what to do.

The author of John prepares us by stressing how much Jesus loved this man and "therefore" stayed where he was two more days. He delayed purposely *so that* he could raise Lazarus, *so that* it would be incontestable that he'd been dead for the accepted four days.

Jesus has raised others from death—the son of the widow of Naim (Lk 7) and the daughter of Jairus (Mk 5)—but they were very recently deceased. A skeptic could argue that they were actually asleep. Patients have been in comas for nearly twenty years, after all. Robert Farrar Capon writes: "They all rise not because Jesus does a number on them, not because he puts some magical resurrection machinery into gear, but simply because he *has that effect on the dead*."

~ *Martha's "rebuke."* It's completely unfair to accuse Martha of weak faith, as one expert puts it: "She regards Jesus as an intermediary who is heard by God, but she does not understand that he is life itself." Of course she doesn't! She lacks two thousand years of theological reflection and as many years of

simplification for ordinary believers. She gave Jesus
what she *had*: "But I know that, even now, God's
power is with you." It might be that she believed Jesus
even now would ask God to raise Lazarus, but her
reaction when he actually does raise Lazarus indicates
that wasn't what she expected.

The psalms are crowded with just such complaints,
and the books of Job and Jeremiah are textbooks for
aspiring grumblers. No one need be ashamed for com-
plaining to God for creating a world where bad things
happen even to good people. The great challenge is
forgiving God for it.

Mary and Martha must have known how dangerous
it had become for Jesus to be in the vicinity of Jerusalem. But like the worthy men who withdrew from the
challenge to stone the adulterous woman, which of us
could blame them for asking him to come despite that?

   ~ *Jesus annoyed*. Commentators haggle over
the meaning of the verb *emebrimasthai* and what
induced the editor to choose it. Normally, it means
"to snort" (connoting displeasure, anger, antagonism).
What makes Jesus annoyed? I tried to suggest he was
displeased—as any teacher would be—when the learn-
ers had given every hint they did understand but, at the
crunch, simply don't comprehend. So often students
can diagram the statement logically, parrot it back on
a quiz or test, but simply don't grasp it, appropriate
it, interiorize it. A crude example might be children
told the dangers of touching a hot stove but not truly
accepting it till they actually get burned, or that credit
cards come due, or that sex is enticing but volatile.

Like all good students, his disciples mouth the
right words about death, but they just don't "get it."
It would probably be fair to say the same about most

Christians and their acceptance of resurrection. A skeptical, clever, insensitive teenager at a wake might say: "If you really—really—believe that resurrection business, why are you crying? That's a contradiction."

The answer is: "Of *course* it's a contradiction! Because I'm a human being, not just a logic machine. No matter what satisfies my mind, this hurts my *heart.* Some day—if you do things right, if you don't let your convictions or your feelings defeat one another—you just might come to understand that."

I suggest also that Jesus—the Son of God, always learning and adapting to being now also fully human—is a touch angry at himself at forgetting for a moment that human emotions are not as logical or as easily accessible as confident convictions.

〜 *The result.* This is the critical moment in the Jesus story. In performing this unthinkable miracle, two miles from the center of opposition, Jesus seals his own death warrant. Although Jesus rightly says that the illness will not end in Lazarus's death, it will surely precipitate his own. No one has greater love than this.

17.

Reclaiming the Temple
MATTHEW 21; MARK 11; LUKE 19; JOHN 2

*J*esus and his Twelve stood on the Mount of Olives across the Kidron valley from the Holy City, spread along a great hill, circled by a monumental four-mile wall spiked with turrets. Reigning at the city's heart, directly across from them, 450 feet above the valley, stood the gleaming, gold-encrusted Temple, home of the Most High.

The valley below them billowed with countless tents; thousands of pilgrims come from all over the world for the Passover at the end of this week.

Jesus, riding a borrowed donkey, seemed cowled in sadness, gazing over at the gigantic walls and the swarms of milling people—colorful foreigners; scarlet-caped soldiers; hawkers with clothes, animals, and souvenirs; beggars; pickpockets; tax collectors in the double-arched Eastern Gate. Someone, most likely one of his own, vaguely aware this was some kind of "moment," shouted just as the blind Jericho beggar had a week before, "Hail, son of David!"

It was combustive. Nearby heads jerked around. It was for just such moment they'd impoverished themselves to come to Jerusalem. To witness a cure. A vision. A story to astound the folks at home. An opening in their wearisome lives for divinity to enter.

All along the road hopeful voices caught it up, "Hail, son of David, our King! King of Israel!" Some pulled down branches from the palm trees, waving them like banners. "Blessed! You come in the name of the Most Holy!"

Two well-dressed men, probably Pharisees, tugged at Jesus's sleeve, "Rabbi. Raise your voice, for the sake of heaven. Tell them to stop. It's too *dangerous*. For *all* of us!"

But Jesus was lifted out of his mood and grinned, "If I tried to silence them," he threw his hand up toward the hulking walls, "those very stones would shout."

The Twelve edged their way through the cacophony of voices—Aramaic, Hebrew, all manners of Latin and Greek, Punic, Coptic, Syriac. Jesus dismounted, and they turned left, into the vast Courtyard of the Gentiles. And there they found the same chaos.

The Hebrew Temple was seven times the size of the entire Roman Forum. Its longer sides were fifteen hundred feet. On either side of the towering central sanctuary, the Holy of Holies and its two lesser chapels, were two enormous open courtyards, each four times the capacity of the Roman Coliseum, ringed by cloisters lined with three rows of Corinthian columns thirty-seven feet high. At feasts like this, the two courtyards could accommodate a quarter million people.

The center block was the Holy of Holies, buttressed at the sides from the massive courtyards by priests' living quarters and fronted by two smaller courts, the outermost allowing purified Hebrew females, the middle one for Hebrew males. The penalty for Gentile trespass was death. Rigid rules also limited all others to the two huge outer courts: those with skin diseases, the disabled, women during their periods, any man after nonreproductive intercourse, tax collectors, bastard sons of priests.

The vast enclosure was jammed with thousands in every manner of dress, some cowed, some curious, others protectively aloof and disdainful. White-robed priests with tubular hats advised foreigners what sacrifices were proper for each need. Guides conducted tours, shouting history, architecture, masonry, lineages. But also all over the huge open area merchants hawked birds and cattle for sacrifice. Rowdy moneylenders bawled out and waved at gullible pilgrims needing to change currency at extortionate rates. The Temple would not accept tainted pagan money for the annual Temple tax. (Less because such coins were defiled by pagan images than that the acceptable Tyrian shekel was better silver and reliable weight.) Great bulls snorted, birds shrieked. The air was spiked with the stink of urine and dung.

Jesus planted his two feet widely and raised his arms in trembling fury.

"*No!*" he shouted.

He reached out a big fist and grabbed a hank of rope hanging from the corner of an awning, toppling the tent and wrapping its flailing occupants and tables. He thrashed right and left.

"*Out!*" he hollered like a madman. He whirled the rope around his shoulders and brought it down, grunting with rage, flipping tables and boxes and coins and abacuses and scales into the air. A few customers and proprietors dropped to their knees, scrounging wildly for the money, heedless of trampling and being trampled by confused and terrified and bellowing bullocks and goats and sheep. He hurled cages of fluttering and screeching birds this way and that, and squadrons of them whirled and soared into the faces of the stampeding people and up into the open sky. Animals and people charged off in every direction, running wildly through the arched colonnades that boxed the enormous plaza.

Slick with sweat, Jesus stopped, trembling, and cried out: "This is my Father's *home*! A house of *prayer*!" "Even for the nations! You've made it a *thieves' bazaar*!"

An outraged Pharisee in black headdress and billowing black robes grabbed one of Jesus's arms forcefully and growled into his face, "How *dare* you?"

Jesus shook him off and glared back, their faces inches apart. "Destroy *this* temple," he snarled, thumping his splayed hands on his chest, "and in three days I will raise it up again."

"You arrogant pig," the Pharisee snapped, spittle spraying his gray beard. "This Temple took forty-six years to build!" He pulled his clothing about him and shoved into the chaos of bodies and screams. The Twelve were completely confused and humiliated by the whole unexpected uproar. It was only much later that any of his people knew what Jesus meant.

Among the thousands of bodies in that vast enclosure, this ruckus was a mere squall, hardly noticeable from the farthest corners. But a squad of Temple police began to plow through the chaos and wreckage. A couple of Jesus's men locked arms with him and forced their way toward the Eastern Gate back to the temporary safety of Bethany.

The officials found this tumultuous civil and religious disobedience—along with the upset of the intruder's unconstrained entry into their city—utterly intolerable. But god sent.

Thoughts to Ponder

～ *Placement*. John places this event very early in Jesus's public life, while the Synoptics—following Mark's earliest sequence—have only a single climactic journey to Jerusalem. The three are probably closer to the truth, since—along with the dramatic news of raising Lazarus—this totally unacceptable assertion of authority impels the ruling hierarchy to put a stop to him. Had he perpetrated such an outrage as early as John's Gospel suggests, it's unlikely he would have lasted three years.

～ *The conquering hero*. Literature is filled with scenes of the triumphant enthronement of kings or the return of the conquering general at the end of a miles-long parade of rich booty and prisoners. But, typically with the Judeo-Christian God, ironies abound. The donkey is only the most obvious, especially a borrowed one. The greatest irony is that this acknowledgment of Jesus's Messiahship and Davidic claim to the throne of Israel is precisely the grounds on which he will be condemned, first by his fellow Jews (blasphemy: "*Are* you the Christ, the Son of the Blessed?") and then by the Roman occupation (sedition: "*Are* you the king of the Jews?")

Worth noting, too, that in the procession of human history this seemingly tumultuous triumph is actually little more than a relatively insignificant fuss on a road to the long-defeated capital of a minor Middle Eastern kingdom. And yet—from the radically broader perspective of a transcendent God—this is the overture to the most significant event since the Creation.

～ *Crowd approval*. It takes very few bumper-sticker battle cries to rouse a protest, especially among a people marginalized and belittled for millennia. They're always ready to mobilize behind any promising rebel. And his adherents are illiterate fishermen, a couple of reformed terrorists, harlots, tax collectors, and a ragtag junta of cured cripples, blind men, and demoniacs. Another highly potent irony is that this crowd receiving them so heartily is the same crowd that, in five days, will we screaming, "Crucify him!" Even his closest devotees will abandon him.

∾ *Pragmatism.* Some commentators try to make a feeble defense of the merchants, arguing that sacrificial animals were integral to the Temple's sacrificial functions, rooted in an ingrained belief in the necessity of atonement—justice rather than mercy. Few of the faithful from all over the known world could afford to bring their own sacrificial animals, and if they did, the Temple priests—who had a vested interest in the process—would almost surely find a blemish in the animal and reject it. So the merchants within the Temple precincts provided an essential service.

But the argument is weak in the face of the many prophets who decried "scapegoats" substituting for genuine conversion of heart. Nor does convenience justify not moving the commerce to the large areas surrounding the Temple. Moreover, there is some diminishment of perspective when a pagan image on a coin is a greater desecration than the uproar of trade, the bellowing and shoving and excrement of animals.

∾ *Reasons* for Jesus's wrath and violent intervention are many. Most obvious is desecration of sacred space, like corralling steers in St. Peter's Basilica. Also, it was blatant profiteering on religion; any pilgrim to Lourdes is repulsed by the cheek-by-jowl shops just outside the gates hawking John XXIII dinner plates and rosary cases that light up in the dark. It was an intrusion on Gentile converts allowed only into that area to pray. What was probably most base was the well-known fact that the purveyors exploited the poor and that the high priest got his cut.

"My Father's house." There is the whole point. In this climactic moment, Jesus is "repossessing" the house of God, which is his birthright. This episode is a flat-out declaration of who Jesus really *is*.

∽ *Authentic worship.* Jesus said: "Go and discover what this means: 'I desire mercy, not sacrifices'" (Mt 9:13). And on March 7, 2015, Pope Francis gave a homily on this story of the cleansing of the Temple.

The disciple of Jesus does not go to church only to observe a precept, to feel okay with a God who should not "trouble" him much. "But I, Lord, go every Sunday, I fulfill . . . , don't mix yourself up with my life, don't bother me." This is the mentality of so many Catholics, so many. The disciple of Jesus goes to church to encounter the Lord and to find in his grace, working in the Sacraments, the strength to think and act according to the Gospel. On which account, we cannot delude ourselves into thinking that we can enter the house of the Lord and "cover ourselves over," with prayers and devotional practices, comportment contrary to the requirements of justice, of honesty or of charity towards our neighbor. We cannot substitute with "religious gifts" what is owed to our neighbor, putting off a true conversion. The cult, the liturgical celebration, are the privileged place to heed the voice of the Lord, which guides us along the road of righteousness and Christian perfection.

∽ *Anger*. This is not the only place in the Gospels where Jesus displays anger. He rebukes Peter for trying to shield him from his mission (Mk 2); just before this Temple episode, for whatever symbolic reasons, he curses a barren fig tree (Mk 11); he's indignant at his men for preventing children from coming to him (Mk 10); he snaps impolitely at demons and lake storms. The entire tirade against the Pharisees in Matthew 23 is evidence enough that there are times when a genuine Christian simply cannot legitimately be reserved. A phrase often credited to Edmund Burke puts it forthrightly: "All that is necessary for the triumph of evil is that good men do nothing."

18.

The Supper

MATTHEW 26:17–35; MARK 14:12–31; LUKE 22:14–38; JOHN 13—17

*I*t was the night of preparation for the Passover, and for whatever reasons, Jesus had decided to celebrate the feast with his group at the very earliest, after sundown the day before. He'd sent Peter and John to set up an upper room he'd arranged for. It was all very puzzling, but Jesus was never far from that. From their camp in Bethany with Lazarus and his sisters, they crossed over the Mount of Olives, down across Kedron Brook, along the southern wall to the southwest gate into the Essene Quarter. Up the narrow street they saw the landlord and his wife waiting for them as they'd been told. They climbed to the second floor and saw a large room with tables and divans arranged in a U-shape in the "Greek way," so all could see the others and the women had access from the front.

All of them made at least a pretense to take the last place. Judas had already taken the seat nearest the door and the stairs. Jesus stood up at the center and began the Kiddush, which the Twelve took up with him:

> Baruch atah, Adonai
> Eloheinu, melech haolam,
> borei p'ri hagafen.

Praise to You, Adonai our God,
Sovereign of the universe,
Creator of the fruit of the vine.

He poured the first cup of remembrance and passed it to the left.

Again he baffled them, interrupting himself. "Just sit at the ends of the couches first. I have a new lesson I want to leave you with."

The word *leave* struck a few of them as odd. Ominous. But also not untypical.

He went to the water jugs and basin by the door, set there for rinsing road dust from the feet. He bent and poured water into the basin and flipped a towel over his shoulder. He crossed the room to the far end of the table. They looked dumbly at one another. He knelt at the feet of Thomas, the farthest from the door, and said, "How I've longed for this moment." He slipped off Thomas's sandals, took his calloused foot in his hand, splashed it with water, and dried it with the towel. Then, the other foot.

Like the slave wealthy people employed for this task for guests at meals, he shuffled on his knees to Matthew, who looked mightily uncomfortable. "So much you don't remember," Jesus said. "So much you'll surely forget. But this . . . what I do tonight I pray you never forget."

He kept moving on his knees from one to the next. They sat in puzzled silence. It wasn't fitting! As if they were noble guests and he their bond slave. Halfway across the long upper table, he looked up fondly at Simon Peter, who drew his feet under him and said, "No, Master. Please. Don't."

Jesus seemed puzzled. "If I don't, Simon, you'll have no place with me."

Peter tried to get his breath. "If so, then do it. And my clumsy hands and foolish head."

Jesus chuckled, "You'll do fine, Simon." He began again, moving along the divans, speaking as he went.

"You call me 'teacher' and 'sir,' which is fitting. But always remember we are different, completely, not like the scribes and Pharisees. They demand reverence, submission. Not us. We are shepherds, not taskmasters. We don't guide with fear of exclusion but with love. Welcoming. Understanding. Eager to serve. That's the lesson to remember. I'm sending you to wash their feet. Remember. That's the way we love our Father."

Near the end, he sat back on his heels. "One of you is ready to betray me."

Voices erupted. "What did he say? . . . Who? . . . Betray? . . . Not me, I swear! . . . *Who?*"

But he held up his hand. "I will not shame him. He could always change his mind." He pushed the bowl of now brown water to the final pair of feet. He eased off Judas's sandals and took his foot in his left hand and bathed it with his right, looking up into the eyes of a man he'd shared everything with for so long. Then he silently bathed the other foot and dried it.

He rose to his feet and took the basin of dirty water and ewer and towel back to where they belonged. He came back to his seat at the top of the table and stood for a quiet moment.

With both hands he reached for the flat bread on the plate before him. "Look at this," he said. "This is my body, broken for you. Take it and eat. Do this so I may stay with you forever."

He tore the bread in halves and passed them right and left. Each one broke off a piece, passed the rest along, and stretched back on his couch. Solemnly. Something important was happening.

He poured the cup of redemption and held it high, saying,

> "Baruch atah, Adonai
> Eloheinu, melech haolam,
> borei p'ri hagafen."

> "Blessed are You, Lord, our God,
>   King of the Universe,
> who creates the fruit of the vine."

"All of you. Look at this. This is a cup of my blood, the blood that ratifies our great new covenant. Drink it."

Instead of passing the cup, he took it first to Thomas and offered it to him, then moved to the next, and the next. Finally, he offered the cup to Judas, who looked at him over the rim as he drank. Jesus whispered quietly to him, "Do what you believe you must."

Judas hesitated, then handed back the cup. He turned and moved quickly to the stairs. Jesus was always sending him on some kind of business.

Night had fallen.

Jesus moved back to his place and set down the cup. "My brothers, I'll be with you like this only a little longer." Murmurs spread around the table. This had become an unsettling meal. "Where I'm going you can't yet come. And there's only one commandment I leave you with. Just one. Love one another. But love the way I have loved you. The way my Father loves. Always forgiving. Always starting over with a new heart. If you remember nothing else, remember that: *love*."

Peter had his dander up about the "leaving." There was nowhere on earth Jesus could go that he couldn't follow. "Master, don't say we can't come!" he pleaded. "I'd follow you *anywhere*. Even through the gates of *death*! You can *never* shake me off!"

Jesus sighed and smiled. "Ah, my great-hearted friend. You mean so well." He took a deep breath. "But, Peter, before tonight's over, before the cock crows, you'll deny you ever knew me. More than once."

Peter sat dumbstruck, hardly breathing. This from a man who seemed to him to know everything!

"But your faith won't fail, my Rock," Jesus said. "It's rooted deep, deep in your great heart. And when you come through the dark time ahead, you'll know how to help your brothers back, too." He kept on. "Brothers, keep your hearts serene, trusting. I'll never truly leave you. I'll be within you when you're most lost, in your loving. You'll never be orphaned."

Jesus closed his eyes and seemed to disappear inside himself, but he spoke his prayer, and they could hear it. "Father, the hour is come. At last. The hour I came for. So through my flesh I can open the way for your glory to flood their souls. So they can grasp why they were made: for eternal life, that they may know you, the one true God and Jesus the Christ whom you have sent.

"I come home to you. So they may come, too. But till then, let them feel the joy that will let them share with me the scorn, the rejection, the torment—but also the freedom. Keep them free from fear. Keep them aware of how precious they are."

He sat quite still for a moment. Then he opened his eyes and stood.

"All right," he said. "It's time."

Thoughts to Ponder

∾ *Fellow servants*. Jesus makes concrete the servant metaphor. It isn't enough to "feel sorry" for the needy—whether physically or materially or spiritually suffering. Empathy must move from the heart into the hands. But take Jesus's intention even further. None of the men at that table was physically ill or impaired, none was impoverished or starving, every one—even Judas—had chucked up his former life in complete surrender to the call of Christ.

One year, meditating on this passage while on retreat, I was tricked by God into switching places from my usual involvement in the scene. Rather than being one of the embarrassed Twelve, God nudged me to take his place. Worse, he suggested I populate the table with the Jesuits in my home community. Oh. I looked up at the first and said, "Of, course. It's a privilege." Then the second: "Well . . . all right." But the third? "I'll be *damned* if . . . !" It was a worthwhile meditation.

Each year when a community reenacts the feet washing, I know I'd find it far *easier* to take the place of Jesus washing than to cringe waiting to *be* served. And yet . . . ? I confess I also feel the chains of self-regard holding me back when I feel impelled to tell others something that hinders their ability to serve even better than they are. Even something as trivial as unpleasant breath or a splotchy suit or dandruff, or monopolizing conversation, or being overly critical. Few—very few—otherwise exemplary Catholics would tell the pastor or deacon his homily doesn't grow in effectiveness with its length and that ideas are linked by more than free association.

∽ *Simon Peter*. He's *not* the ideal disciple, just the usual one. You can get an excellent insight into what Jesus, the Founder of Christianity, expected a pope or bishop or priest to be by tracing Peter's actions and reactions. Pope Francis seems to be doing superlatively well at being the priest/bishop/pope Jesus led us all to expect, or at least hope for.

There was nothing "small" about St. Peter. Nether he nor any of the others was an academic—much less an expert in canon law or any other kind of law. He was impetuous, hearty, quite likely too loud, devoted, but easily cowed. Later, as the fledgling church's leader, he was humble enough to admit he was wrong about two matters he'd thought essentials of the faith: circumcision and dietary laws. He yielded to Paul, the theologian—who was smarter, but only in a different way. He was the kind of man who could say to a crippled beggar after the Pentecost whirlwind and fire: "I have no silver or gold, but what I have I give you; in the name of Jesus Christ of Nazareth, stand up and walk" (Acts 3:6).

∾ *The Real Presence.* Perhaps the single most important reason I am a Catholic, rather than some other kind of Christian, is my unshakable belief in transubstantiation, that—*somehow*—the bread and wine truly *become* the Body and Blood of Christ. I can give no rational, left-brain proof for that belief, other than my conviction that the God who could make a universe out of nothing can do anything he damn well pleases. Nor can I explain *how* such a transformation can occur, any more than I can explain how the universe came from nothing. I can no more explain it than I can explain why I have remained a Jesuit for sixty years or my friends can explain why they married and stayed together through thick and thin. I just know, implacably, that it is *right*.

Protestant theologian Karl Barth articulates what a difference it makes to believe that the presence of the risen Lord actually is in not only the assembly and in God's word and in the priest but actually *in* the bread and wine:

At those times when the task of being ministers of the divine word, as we of the Reformed Churches say, has oppressed us, have we not all felt a yearning for the rich services of Catholicism, and for the enviable role of the priest at the altar? When he elevates the *Sanctissimum*, with its full measure of that meaning and power which the *material* symbol enjoys over the symbol of the human word, the double grace of the sacrificial death and the incarnation of the Son of God is not only preached in words but actually takes place in his hands.

In the next note on Judas, I quote John 6, in which Jesus spoke of the Eucharist; many disciples balked at actually eating Christ's flesh and drinking his blood. Many of the persecutors of the earliest church did so under the righteous motive of obstructing cannibalism. As we need to remind ourselves again and again, these disciples were hearing those words for the *first* time.

And no matter how many arguments pro and con, no matter how many anathemas and counter-anathemas Christians have hurled at one another, scripture quotes Jesus as saying: "*Gar sarx mou alethes esti brosis, kai to haima mou alethes esti posis,*" "My flesh is true food and my blood is true drink." Unequivocally. Flat out. Not "let this stand for" or "let this always remind you." Jesus says: *alethes,* which the Greek dictionary defines as "what cannot be hidden, undeniable reality when fully tested, i.e., it will ultimately be shown to be *fact.*"

Or as the great Flannery O'Connor put it more pithily: "If it's only a symbol, then I say t'hell with it."

Long before Jesus, Socrates said that the first requisite for finding the truth is humility, that only those are wise who are certain they're not, that they *don't* have the final answer, about anything, and never will. That's a truth I assume all the theologians and officials accept, but I wonder if sometimes they might forget.

～ *Judas Iscariot.* Jesus was no fool. To think that the most astute man who ever lived would have picked as one of a limited dozen closest companions the caricature Judas of the common imagination is unthinkable. Judas was not only competent but dedicated. Earlier, Jesus had posed a totally mystifying and repugnant requirement for joining him:

> "Very truly, I tell you, unless you eat the flesh of the Son of Man and drink his blood, you have no life in you. Those who eat my flesh and drink my blood have eternal life, and I will raise them up on the last day; for my flesh is true food and my blood is true drink." (Jn 6:53–55)

Because of this many of his disciples turned back and no longer went about with him. So Jesus asked the Twelve, "Do you also wish to go away?" Simon Peter answered him, "Lord, to whom can we go? You have the words of eternal life. We have come to believe and know that you are the Holy One of God."

But despite this unspeakable demand, despite their lack of twenty centuries' attempts to make the Eucharist less difficult for uneducated people to accept, these twelve stayed with him. Even Judas.

Why the betrayal, though? After all the miracles, all the lessons that violence would never carry the day or ever bring peace, why did Judas so suddenly and totally change? I find the simple explanation in John's Gospel too glib and otherwise unsubstantiated: "He was a thief; he kept the common purse and used to steal what was put into it" (12:6). Jesus was sharp. If it was a habit with Judas, why wouldn't Jesus have stopped it? And why not give the purse to Matthew/Levi, who was a professional accountant and tax collector?

I take my cue from Dorothy Sayers's fine series of radio plays for the BBC collected as *The Man Born to Be King*. Her theory is Judas, like Simon the Zealot, had been a freedom fighter, like a member of the IRA, provoking the Romans and fomenting armed resistance. She argues that Jesus had *really* converted Judas, as thoroughly as Saul into Paul. But the events of that final weekend were too much for him. The *royal* entry into the city and the people's acclaiming him king—and Jesus *not stopping* it. Then his totally atypical violence in the Temple. Sayers suggests that Judas—perhaps the only one who truly understood and accepted Jesus's completely countercultural message—now completely misread Jesus's ironic purposes on Palm Sunday. It was as if Che Guevara suddenly caught Fidel Castro conniving with bankers in Zurich and New York, or like Biff Loman catching his adored father, Willy, in a hotel room with a hooker. Sayer believed Judas turned Jesus over to the authorities to save him from himself, from betraying the gentle revolution. He did it as an act of love. I can buy that.

∾ *Judas and the Eucharist.* St. John Chrysostom, St. Augustine, and St. Thomas Aquinas all agree that Jesus shared the Eucharist with Judas, even knowing what he was about to do. John's Gospel has no explicit description of the institution of the Eucharist. Matthew and Mark are unclear (unless he slipped out unnoticed between verses). But Luke offers a route to a more irenic insight into Jesus, though he places a burden on the self-righteous who see Satan entering Judas, thus placing him beyond redemption. Luke says—*after* the Eucharist (22:14–20)—in the next verse, "But see, the one who betrays me is with me, and his hand is on this table" (22:21).

Any Christian shocked at the possibility of Jesus sharing his flesh and blood with Judas has probably missed his utter lack of refinement in treating sinners everywhere in the Gospels. Not to mention that he undeniably shared the Eucharist with Peter and the others when he clearly knew Peter would deny him and every one of the others would desert him too.

According to Jesus—in the Parable of the Weeds (Mt 13) and in his description of the last judgment (Mt 25)—the question of worthiness defies any definitive assessments until long after we're all gone. And, according to the same authoritative source, the elements of the evaluation will have nothing to do with disciplinary questions but rest solely on sensitivity to those in need.

19.

The Apostate Pope
MATTHEW 26; MARK 14; LUKE 22; JOHN 18

*I*t was well after midnight. The *seder* meal had gone on for hours. Jesus spoke on and on, as if he were never going to be able to teach them again. He'd been so frightening, talking of being betrayed, deserted. More disturbing because he'd been so *calm* about it. He'd spoken of his being *the* way to his Father, and he promised that, when he was "gone," some new Spirit would take his place (as if that were possible). He spoke again of his being like a vine, the source of life and power in them now. Or in the future sometime. And he'd prayed, aloud, for them, and said they were to be gloried. But not the way they'd hoped. And that even if they forgot everything he'd said—and they would—this Spirit would remind them of everything again. And a great deal that they'd already forgotten.

Then, despite the fact they were all yawning and yearning just to turn over on the couches and sleep awhile, Jesus insisted they go to their usual place in the garden on Olivet to pray! In the darkest hours of the night.

So they stumbled along behind him down the street to the gate, out across the south wall and across Kedron again, past the silent pilgrim tents, and up into the olive grove where they often came to pray. He told most of them to sit by the opening to the grove and watch. For what? In the dead of night? But he took his favorites further into the trees—Peter, of course, and the Zebedee brothers, James and John. Then he went a bit further, by himself. And he fell to his knees like a man struck hard from behind.

Which is about all they remembered. A couple were roused by Jesus's voice, talking to the three special ones, sounding wounded, disappointed. They tried to catch more, but they were pulled back into sleep by dull fatigue.

Then one or two of the light sleepers, Thomas for one, felt the tang of smoke and pitch in his nose and sat up, completely alert like a guard dog. Through the gnarled olive trees they saw a line of fire drawing near. There were a couple of Roman soldiers, a couple of Temple police with swords, a ragtag bunch of nighthawk ne'er-do-wells with clubs along for the adventure. And in the lead, their brother, Judas.

Jesus pushed his way through them and stood a moment, quietly. Judas closed the space between them, put both his hands on Jesus's shoulders, looked into his eyes, and kissed his mouth.

Jesus whispered so quietly only the closest could hear, "With a kiss?"

Then, ignoring Judas, he said to the Jewish officer, "Whom are you looking for?"

The grizzled Temple veteran snapped, "Jesus of Nazareth."

"I am he," Jesus said.

A couple of the Temple guards stepped back and fell to the ground.

Fool that he was, Simon Peter rushed through with his long dagger drawn and slashed at the high priest's slave, lopping off his ear. Jesus stepped forward, pulled

Peter back by the shoulder, and said, "No more of *that*!" He shoved Peter back with the others.

With utter calm, he bent down and picked up the bloody ear. He bent to the slave who lay there moaning and holding the side of his head. Jesus placed the ear, then pulled his hand away, and in the gore, the ear was sealed in place. Those in the arresting party were less confident than they had been.

Jesus spoke to them again. "Am I a bandit, that you come out for me with swords and clubs? Day after day, I sat in the Temple teaching. Why not then and there? Ah, witnesses!" He reached out his wrists for the ropes. "I'm the one you want. Let these men go."

A Temple guard with a rope stepped forward, and his movement triggered a stampede of feet. Every one of Jesus's men fled into the night.

And they led Jesus away.

Later Jesus was trooped into the palace of the high priest where, despite the midnight hour, a quorum of the High Council, the Sanhedrin, had been convoked by Caiphas, the high priest. In the courtyard below servants who'd been rousted from sleep to prepare the banquet hall for their highly unusual gathering and the squad of Temple guards who'd brought the prisoner were warming themselves at a charcoal fire in the courtyard. They'd all been told to be ready for any eventuality. It was nearly dawn, and there was little chance of getting back to bed.

Among them, warming his hands, stood Simon Peter, his eyes darting about like a skittery pigeon. The old woman next to him, wrinkled as a walnut, cocked an eye and snorted, "An' who're you, big fella?"

Peter tried to shrink into himself. "Just a man. Out in the cold."

"You're a hillbilly, ain't cha? The accent. Galilee?"

Peter was silent, wishing her dead. But he couldn't bring himself to desert. Again.

The hag stretched her ropy neck and pointed her chin at him. "*Right*! Last week. The big fuss on the East Gate. Him on the donkey. You was right there with him, wasn't cha?"

"You don't know *anything*," Peter snapped. "I never saw that man before in my *life*!" He turned from the fire and moved away, closer to the street. But he held there, unable to leave.

One of the Temple police sidled up to him at the gate. "If I was you, friend, and I knew even that poor bastard's great grandma, I'd haul ass back to the hills right quick."

"Sir, I *swear* to you! That old bitch is *crazy*. I don't *know* him!"

The old crone wasn't ready to let it go. She came from the fire and snagged the guard by his cloak. "I *never* forget a face, Motek. He's one o' them hillbilly rebels."

Peter raised his arm to backhand her, but he held himself, his chest heaving. "*Damn* you! Will you leave me *alone*? I *swear*, by *heaven*, I do . . . not . . . *know* that bastard!"

Just then, from somewhere nearby, over the roofs came the coo-coo-ca-rooo of a rooster heralding daybreak. Peter suddenly froze where he stood. "Before the cock crows . . . "

He turned into the street and began to run. Sobbing. And he wept. And he wept.

Thoughts to Ponder

⌒ *Judas's* main usefulness to the authorities was to lead them to Jesus in a place where his arrest wouldn't cause a disturbance that could ripple out into something serious. It's possible that the arrest was delayed so long after Judas left the supper because he'd taken them first to the upper room and only then to the place they had often gone to pray.

This kiss is one of those scriptural occurrences where one says, "If this didn't actually happen, it *should* have." It is an act indescribably beyond mere hypocrisy. Yet it can't have been the cold-blooded caricature of Judas that Dorothy Sayers said was an insult to Jesus's intelligence. What was happening inside him? Try to imagine your way into the maelstrom inside Judas.

Only Matthew reports that Judas hanged himself. He and Peter had both severed themselves from Jesus, Judas more decisively, but both dramatically. Judas's betrayal was clearly calculated and Peter's impulsive, unplanned. But the difference was that Peter hung on. Quite likely, Judas was the more clever of the two. But Peter's connection to Jesus was far more profound.

~ *Peter.* An apostate is one who renounces a religious or moral belief and commitment—a traitor, defector, renegade, deserter. Samaritans were apostates from Judaism; so were several Hebrew kings, like Ahab who drifted into Canaanite fertility cults. During the early persecutions many died rather than deny Christ, but many were not so firmly rooted. Throughout its two thousand year history, the church has been torn again and again by individuals and groups hurling the accusation of apostasy at one another.

But few cases are clearer than Simon Peter, who quite unequivocally, publicly, and under oath denied any association with Christ. What's more, even if his denial was triggered by fear, he did it three times in one night, with at least some time between to reflect.

And his sellout was not to a soldier with a knife at his throat or to torturers but to a *bystander*.

The fact that the early church did not hesitate to record the cowardly defection of its most significant figure makes a very strong case for its credibility. But far more important than Peter's sin—in the eyes of the one Christians believe is God himself—is his *loving*. Not just that he loved Jesus, as he so fiercely did. But—even more difficult—he trusted that *Jesus* loved *him*.

And at the end, the coward of the high priest's courtyard was crucified rather than deny his experience of Christ, crucified and risen.

Peter stands foursquare as unyielding evidence there is *no* sin beyond God's total forgiveness—provided we trust in the bottomless love God has for each of us. If only merciful doctrines were as consistently and powerfully promoted as the sin part, the faith we offer might more often appear to ordinary people as good news. Today, even the "sin part" seems to have ceased.

Peter is an adult who does, truly, embody Jesus's desire that in order to enter the kingdom we must be born again, take on the attitudes of a child, work less from our heads than from our hearts. Like a child, he trusted that he was loved. He didn't reason to it. He submitted to it.

My friend Jeff Gillenkirk sent me a poem written by Georgetown professor Roland Flint. It shows not only who Peter was but how different the real Jesus was—and is—from the holy-card Jesus:

Follow

Now here is this man mending his
    nets
after a long day, his fingers

nicked, here and there, by ropes and
     hooks,
pain like tomorrow in the small of his
     back,
his feet blue with his name, stinking
     of baits,
his mind on a pint and supper—noth-
     ing else—
a man who describes the settled shape
of his life every time his hands
make and snug a perfect knot.
I want to understand, if only for the
     story,
how a man like this,
a man like my father in harvest,
like Bunk MacVane in the stench of
     lobstering,
or a teamster, a steelworker,
how an ordinary working stiff,
even a high tempered one,
could just be called away.
It's only in one account
he first brings in a netful—
in all the others, he just calls,
they return the look or stare and then
they 'straightaway' leave their nets to
     follow.
That's all there is. You have to figure
what was in that call, that look.
(And I wouldn't try it on a tired
     working man
unless I was God's son—
he'd kick your ass right off the pier.)
If they had been vagrants,

poets or minstrels, I'd understand
    that,
men who would follow a different
    dog.
But how does a man whose move-
    ment,
day after day after day,
absolutely trusts the shape it fills
put everything down and walk away?
I'd pass up all the fancy stunting
with Lazarus and the lepers
to see that one.

20.

The Death of God
MATTHEW 27; MARK 15; LUKE 23; JOHN 19

*I*s was nearly noon before the charade of the two trials was out of the way. Both trials were essential, of course, to pacify the emotional mob. They had to grasp that the hero they simple-mindedly hailed the previous weekend was a charlatan, an apostate, and a revolutionary.

The first trial took place before the High Council, the Sanhedrin, on the charge of blasphemy, making himself equal to God. Held in the dead of night, it was somewhat illegal but was rectified with a quick meeting just after dawn. A wearying parade of feckless witnesses testified at cross purposes that the Nazarene carpenter, Jesus, had claimed he was going to tear down the Temple. Not only that, but he would rebuild it in three days. Which—with only a dozen hillbilly fishermen and a few other hangers-on, malcontents, and undisciplined women—was highly unlikely. But that mob when he came into the city was unpredictable.

Then some witness testified that he meant that he *himself* was the Temple *they* were going to destroy, which would have certified him as a madman but hardly qualified for getting rid of him completely. That seemed verified by another witness and came close to a charge: equating his own value to the holiest place on earth, the divine residence. Then—through the intervention of the Most High—the impasse solved itself. Caiphas the high priest was inspired to put the accused under oath and asked, pointblank: "*Are* you the Messiah? *Are* you the Son of the Most High?"

And right there, in front of about seventy unimpeachable witnesses, he said, "I AM!"

He spoke the unspeakable: the name of God! About himself. Dumbstruck by the defendant's arrogance, the high priest ripped the front of his tunic, as did the other worthy elders of the nation. With only one or two abstaining, the verdict was death.

However, the Roman occupation denied subjugated peoples the death penalty, which necessitated a second trial before the disdainful governor, Pontius Pilate. Since blasphemy to their sand-blasted God was of no concern to him, they deftly transformed the charge to insurrection, organizing a seditious march into the capital in which the mob named him king of the Jews in defiance of Caesar. That engaged the governor's profound self-interest.

Pilate dallied with the prisoner awhile, tweaking the pious noses of the backwater clergy, but eventually they outmaneuvered him by hinting some fool might find reason to report him to Rome for releasing a proven insurrectionist. So, ignoring the irony, he released a genuine insurrectionist named Barabbas and yielded the prisoner to their pleasure. He would supply a squad of soldiers to keep order; they'd supply the executioners and wherewithal. He washed his hands of anything more.

As they left the Roman Praetorium, two more rebels were added to the tawdry parade pushing through the irate proprietors of the stalls along the narrow roadway. The rebel-preacher fell once or twice under the weight of the six-foot crosspiece, which held things up a bit, but to give him credit, he kept getting up again. The third time the centurion in charge of the guard lost patience and made some hick pilgrim from Africa carry one end of the beam. That sped things up.

They left the city by the Damascus gate into Golgotha, the Skull place or Calvaria, as the Romans called it. A gully stretched outside the north wall, a played-out quarry with convenient niches and caves used for quick burials of the well-to-do. At the far end was a knob of rock that gave the place its name. On the top several upright eight-foot posts jutted up for crucifixions. Anyone sent to hell from here was buried in the potter's field south of the city.

The sorry procession worked its way up the skull hill and let the condemned men collapse under the rough-hewn timbers they'd carried. The spectators stayed at a distance. The executioners stripped the three men, leaving their loincloths for propriety. Tougher on the preacher. He'd been lashed bloody, and his tunic had sealed itself to his skin. Later, the soldiers would dice for whatever in the pile was more than rags.

The soldier handlers shoved a sponge at each victim's mouth. It was laced with some drug to ease the pain of the spikes in their wrists and ankles. Less from concern for the crucified than for the nerves of those stuck with the rotten task of doing it. The two rebels sucked the sponges greedily. The preacher spat it out. The carpenters hauled the crossbars to the stony soil above the men's shoulders, stretched out their arms, and measured the beam to augur a starting hole in the right spot. No one used ropes anymore. Too much time, and the bodies sagged, so they took longer to die. The executioners knew their craft.

The nails were spikes as long as a woman's hand, planted into the wrists and ankles where the nest of bones would hold the limbs from slipping out. The two terrorists screamed like the damned, but Jesus, the Nazarene, held it in. Part of the soldiers' job was to lift the prisoner and the crossbar up to the top of the upright, the reason for its low height. They grunted with the weight, but they were strong men who'd done this before. The carpenters quickly hammered a spike into a slanted hole at the back to secure it from slipping.

As a final tweak to the priests Pilate had an inexpert soldier letter a crude banner to tack along the bar of Jesus's cross. Some was hidden by his head and the spiked crown, but it said "Jesus the Nazarene, King of the Jews" in four languages, so no one could misread his crime. Or the implication: "This is the best of the Jews."

And then the true tedium began. Some poor bastards lasted a week. But the duty roster changed. It was a living.

Jesus sagged, the whole weight of his body shrieking pain to his wrists. Flies drank his blood and tears. His nose had been broken hours before, one eye was swollen shut, both were purple and yellow. There was not enough space in his body to contain the pain. His fingers spasmed involuntarily, and he had to dig deeply into himself in order to breathe. In agony he lifted his head upright and shouted, "Father! *Forgive* them! They don't know what they're doing!"

The Aramaic meant nothing to the soldiers, so they started to toss for the rebels' rags. But it disquieted the Jewish carpenters.

One of the rebels hanging in agony next to Jesus lifted his head and barked in Jesus's direction, "Hey, Messiah! Hey you! Messiah! Whyn't cha pull a fast one, huh? Get cherself down, huh? And take me 'n' lamehead Dismas wit' cha! Goddamn! I'll worhip ya *myself*!"

The other rebel growled almost inaudibly, "Shut your face, asshole!"

The first one gargled, "Come over and make me, numbnuts!"

The second one waited for breath. Somehow he had to speak. "Leave the poor hick *be*, you pig. He didn't do nothin'! Can't you do *one* damn descent thing before we go t' hell?"

"God ain't stupid, Diz," the first one snapped and went quiet.

The second rebel tried to turn toward the middle cross. "Jesus," he rasped. "Good luck, pal. When you . . . when you get . . . to this . . . kingdom . . . " He dug for air. "Remember me?"

"Today," Jesus gasped. "You'll . . . be with . . . me. My word!"

For a while there was silence on the hill and out into the quarry where onlookers lurked in the sparse shade of the scrubby bushes. Many had already left. Nothing interesting anymore, and there was the Passover to get ready. So gradually that few noticed it, the midday sky began to turn gray and go dark, as if a sandstorm from the south were closing in very high in the sky. Heat lightning slashed through the uncanny darkness at noon. But there was no hope of rain.

Several women and a man had edged to the foot of the central cross, and Jesus seemed to speak in gasps to them. Most of the soldiers dozed in the heat. The executioners had long since departed; one Jewish carpenter stayed to supervise the removals.

Suddenly there came a convulsive crack of thunder, and everyone on the hill and in the ravine jolted to attention. But as the echo rolled off, only the weak voice of Jesus cried out, *"Eli! Eli! Eli!"*

One of the youngest soldiers ran to soak a rag from the pile with wine from his bottle and fix it to the top of his javelin, but another one held him back. "No, wait! That's the name of their god. Maybe there'll be a show!"

Jesus's mouth gaped open and he screamed: *"Eli, Eli, lama sabachthani!"*

The centurion shook the carpenter's shoulders. "What's he *saying*? Is it a *curse*?"

The carpenter beat his breast and trembled, " He's saying . . . he's saying . . . 'My God, My God, why have you forsaken me?'"

The young soldier thrust up his javelin and poked the wine-soaked rag at Jesus's lips. And Jesus sucked at the moisture, the last drops of the cup he had prayed God would take from him. It was enough to be able to speak.

"Father," he rasped, "into your hands I offer my soul." Then, in a whisper, "It's *done!*"

His tormented lungs went still.

The hard-bitten centurion looked up at the corpse. "Now there was a son of a god."

The soldiers had packed up and gone. The onlookers had drifted away. The quarry was empty except for the few women, the young man, and—to their astonishment—two highly placed Hebrew elders, Sanhedrin members. One named Nicodemus had his servants bring a ladder, a linen shroud, and a huge supply of spiced burial ointments. The anointing would have to wait a day, since the Sabbath and Passover began in only an hour or so. The other man was named Joseph, from Arimathea, some upcountry town, who believed Jesus and had offered Jesus's mother his newly purchased tomb-cave so Jesus would not be buried with the other two in the potter's field.

Two of the elders' servants mounted the ladder, slung the long shroud under the arms of the corpse and over the crossbeam. Others on tiptoes prised out the spikes, and they slowly lowered the body and lapped it in the linen. The men shouldered the corpse and moved down the quarry slope to the rock wall where the small niche opened at the top of a low rise. The women followed silently, noting the place so they could return after the Sabbath to do things properly.

The servants laid the body on a shelf just inside the small cave and came out. The small group of men and women stood mutely a moment. Then they helplessly nodded to one another and went their separate ways to await the worst Sabbath of their lives.

They had had such hopes.

Thoughts to Ponder

~ *The Trials* were both foregone shams, each engineered by shallow self-interest. But, meditating on Jesus as he stood there silent before the sneering, self-righteous elders and then the toughly pragmatic pagan governor, treated like a tethered animal, one oughtn't to miss the meaning of the moment: God utterly humiliated.

A frighteningly bright ten-year-old boy named Cisco, who had been to all the Holy Week ceremonies with his parents, asked me a frighteningly bright question: "Father, if God loved his only Son as much as they say, why did he make him die such an awful death?"

After all these years, have you an answer?

The only one I could offer—since I refused to accept it as atonement in the usual sense—was this: "To show us how it's done, Cisco. With dignity."

~ *Forsaken.* Way back in Edom, six centuries before Christ, old Job was bereft of his children and all his wealth, deserted by his wife, crusted with scabs, exhausted by the empty answers from his know-it-all friends. He could have looked up at Yahweh at the end of God's whirlwind speech about Job's inescapable ignorance, daring to challenge God's reasons for making him suffer—for no reasons Job was capable of comprehending. Job could well have said, "You do *understand* everything, yes? You have reasons beyond my capacity to fathom. You know my pain, but only as I knew the pain of my wife's childbirths. You are too perfect to know how this *feels*! Not just the agony in my flesh but in my *soul*. Do you know how this *feels*?"

Here, in the banquet hall of the high priest, on the porch of the Roman Presidium, spiked to a cross on Skull Hill, God himself *can* look down at Job. And at each of us in our loneliness, rejection, physical pain, temptation to give up. And God *can* say, "Yes, my loyal friend. Yes. Now I *do* know pain. Not merely understand. But I *feel* it, too."

I can rejoice in a God who has felt godforsaken.

~ *Atonement.* Just as Job, repelled by the theological "answers" to his suffering offered by his pious, learned friends, I finally found courage to admit my refusal to accept the "justifications" of Jesus's sufferings (and by extension Job's sufferings and my own) as "atonement" to a God immovably offended by a single sin before history began.

First, how can God be blissfully perfect *and* bedeviled by a millennial grudge?

Second, the whole economic metaphor of an infinite "debt" may appeal to accountants but not to people like Job, who considered God his friend, not a loan-shark.

Third, ransom is demanded only by a hostile power, not by the God that Jesus revealed as the father of the prodigal son, or the Jesus/God who dealt with whores, adulteresses, embezzling stewards, crooked tax men, and a dozen apostate apostles in a diametrically opposite way.

Fourth, too many ignore the fact that, according to the recollections of privileged witnesses who chose to die rather than deny their experience, the *first* thing Jesus/God cried out from his place of execution was, "Father, *forgive* them! They don't know what they're doing!"

Fifth, this Jesus—to whom both my professors and I had vowed our lives—when asked by Peter how often we must forgive, replied (perfectly consistent with his character): "Seventy times seven times." If God suggests 490 acts of forgiveness—*each* time—wouldn't that justify the hope that we can expect the same leniency from a God to whom we also ascribe infinite mercy?

I don't deny the doctrine of atonement. I simply must confess my ignorance of any argument that can justify it.

The crucifixion, understood as a cosmic act of loving forgiveness, "says" that our Creator has allowed himself/herself/themselves to become so incurably smitten with us that God wants very, very much to forgive. But forgiveness simply can't occur until the injuring party *also* wants it. But as the archetypal Parable of the

Prodigal Son demonstrates, all we have to do is turn for home and our Father will come *running*!

      Now it's done. Despite scriptural references to Jesus's submitting "like a sheep, dumb before the shearers" (Is 53:7), this was not stoic, nerveless compliance. It was a willed *acceptance* of the Father's will—which was assuredly *unclear* to Jesus in Gethsemane: "'*Abba*, Father,' he said, 'everything is possible for you. *Take* this cup from me. Yet not what I will, but what you will'" (Mt 26:39). He said he was willing to take whatever the Father chose to send. And he really *meant* it. When he taught us to pray "thy will be done," he asked us to really *mean* it. Even when we don't understand. At the end Jesus cried out, close to despair. But at the last he freely surrendered his spirit. To his father. And to us.

21.

Breakfast by the Lake

JOHN 21

𝒟awn had just begun to lighten the mist that hovered over the slate-slick lake. Seven of the apostles were dully stroking Peter's boat to shore. It had been Simon Peter's idea the night before. Suddenly standing, he announced, "I'm going to fish." The other six—Thomas, Nathaniel the kid from Cana, the Zebedee brothers, a couple more—heaved to their feet and followed. Anything was better than sitting around waiting for someone to tell them what to do.

So they'd rowed for hours in the dead dark, dropping the net in all the right places. Nothing but water and weeds and rowing, rowing. A couple bailed. Simon's boat had always leaked. But doing this for the whole night was worse than doing nothing.

About a hundred yards or so from shore, John looked across the shallows and saw a figure through the thinning haze, silhouetted against a low fire.

They heard a familiar voice. "No luck, lads?"

"Nothing," a few grunted back, stroking listlessly.

Jesus called, "Throw the net off the right side. Better luck there."

Not sure they weren't imagining the whole thing, they obeyed.

Suddenly, they felt the net plunge, burning their calloused palms, as if some force were herding fish into the net. It strained the heavy muscles of their arms and shoulders. Awkwardly, piece by piece, they tugged off their sweaty, constricting clothes, till they all worked near naked.

"Pull! Get your backs into it," Simon barked, as if they weren't already doing that. The net was snapping cords here and there, far too heavy to haul over the gunnels, so they hung the net at the stern and took to the oars again, towing the swollen load behind them.

John and Simon Peter were at the foremost oars, near the prow. John elbowed Peter and said, "Look. It's him."

Peter stepped his oar and peered. "Who?"

"The Master," John whispered. "Our Lord."

"Do you think?"

"Who else could it be?"

"Oh," Peter whispered. "Oh." Ever since that morning when the Master had simply . . . appeared to them, in that room, back in the city, when he impossibly had come back again, each next time stopped Peter's heart. As unnerving as the first. And not a whisper of what Peter had done that awful night.

"Someone should . . . ," Peter stammered and fumbled for his clothes. Slick with sweat, he punched his arms into his tunic and stepped onto the gunnel to jump in, heedless of the depth or the fact the sodden tunic would weigh him down. Much more aware of what was proper. He surfaced spluttering and stroked toward the shallows, then sloshed to his feet in the shallows, and the others shipped the oars and dragged in the skiff and the net.

Like someone intoxicated, Peter stumbled, dripping, across the pebbles and dropped to his knees, and Jesus cupped Peter's chin in his hands. Peter's heart thumped heavily. Behind the two of them, the others saw red-gold coals and smelled seared fish and flatbread baking. Jesus pulled Peter to his feet and said, "Bring some more."

Peter joined the others, hauling the ungainly net onto the beach and spilling the great silver pile. Out of habit, Levi began to separate and count the great heaps—153 large fish—plump Biny fish, tilapia, bushels of wriggling sardines.

"Come eat your breakfast," Jesus said, and gestured them 'round the charcoal fire. Sheets of slate were balanced over the embers, covered with gutted fish and strips of lumpy batter.

Not one of them dared ask, "Is it really you?" They knew it was the Lord. No matter how impossible, it still was. But somehow he was more alive even than before. His mere presence made their flesh tingle. Jesus took the bread and tore it for them. And the same with the fish. And he brought it around to each of them, his eyes lingering on each of their eyes.

They sat quietly and ate. They knew.

When they had their fill, they sprawled around the dying fire. It was just as it had been for three years. Companionable. Secure. Only so different now. They could never shed the memory that they had all run. Deserted him. Peter the worst.

From the quiet came Jesus's voice. "Simon?"

Peter jolted upright. "Yes, Lord." He *knew* it was coming. Had to.

"Simon," Jesus cocked his head quizzically. "Are you my true friend? Even if the others should fail me?"

Peter clutched his fists at his big chest like a child. "Oh, yes, Lord. Truly. You know I am."

"Then I want you to feed my little ones, the weak ones, my lambs."

For a moment it was quiet. Only the soft gurgle of waves nibbling the sand.

Then, Jesus said it again. "Simon?"

Oh, God! Peter began to tremble. Now it would come out. The poison. But it *did* have to come out. He knew that.

"Simon? Do you love me?"

Peter was close to tears. "Oh, Lord. You *know* I do!"

"Then feed my sheep, too. I want it to be you."

Peter was trying to heave up a breath, but he could only huff. This was not the way he feared, not as painful as it should be. Not painful. Terrifying.

The silence cloaked them all again.

And the third time, like salt to a wound, Jesus said, "Simon, are you sure? Are you sure you are my true, loyal friend?"

The tears spilled down Peter's cheeks into his beard. His heart felt bruised with the Master's kindness. "Oh, Lord! You know *everything*! You can read my innermost heart. You *know* I love you, truly, to the bottom of my soul!"

"Then," Jesus said, "I want you to be for them what I've been for you. A good shepherd."

Peter had no remote idea what that meant, but, whatever it was, he was ready to try his best at it. No matter how poor his best was.

Jesus nodded. "Yes. You'll surely do. Remember when you were a boy, how proud you were to be able to dress yourself, to go wherever you had a mind to go? No more. Their needs will now govern yours. And when you're old, you will be tied down as I was and finally follow me."

They settled into silence. Trying to understand.

Thoughts to Ponder

∾ Some dither over the suddenness of Peter's *decision* to fish and to do it at night. Anybody who's stood by Peter at any point in the Gospels knows he's a rambunctious man, not a deliberate scholar. And, of course, night was the time the fish fed, and they could be sold fresh-caught early in the morning.

∾ They had *caught nothing* because now—as fishers of souls—they could never get started without Jesus, much less succeed. The same hidden lesson emerged when Peter was incapable of walking on water unless he kept his eyes on Jesus.

∾ *John.* Despite my lack of the gospel writers' divine validation, I made an editorial decision (as they often did) to specify this Gospel's use of "the Beloved Disciple" to John the apostle. There is such a dispute about who this personage could be that I thought it would be a useless distraction for a modern reader.

∾ *Master/Lord.* Since the resurrection, the community now sees Jesus as far more than just their teacher.

∾ *Peter's clothes.* Some find this puzzling. It doesn't make any sense to put *on* clothes to jump into ten feet of water. But it makes sense if you know Simon Peter: impetuous, leading with his heart and gut and not his head. (A hint once more for all churchfolk.) With no critical thinking, Peter *knows* someone should do *something* to show respect and reverence for the Lord. Like all well-brought-up country boys, he knows what's *proper.*

He was quite likely stripped down to his loincloth. The night may have been cool, but the work was strenuous, and there was no one around to shock. But his nakedness also "fits" here. This is the third time (at least) they've encountered Jesus returned. And apparently nothing has been said about Peter's apostasy—denying Christ within hours of the last supper. Peter's soul is not just naked. It's a raw, open wound. What adult hasn't been there?

~ *Charcoal fire.* Previously in John's Gospel (18:18), at Peter's denial, we find him in the high priest's courtyard mingling with the servants at a charcoal fire, denying Christ with unprintable oaths. The similarity is surely intentional.

~ *Number of fish.* If the editor intended to make some symbolic point, he did it so cleverly no modern critic can be sure what it was, nor is it likely his original readers could have. But it is so specific, it does seem purposeful. One reason is that the number and size (some Biny fish weigh up to fifteen pounds) suggest that the net *should* have broken, so the emphasis is likely symbolic of the variety and size of souls the ideal church can accommodate.

St. Jerome (d. 420) claimed Greek zoologists had identified 183 as the total number of fish species, which has as valid a claim as any other. Another is that—like the endearing (and typical) detail of Peter's putting on clothes before jumping into the water to be "proper"—the detail is someone's actual remembrance of the moment. But like the abundance of the loaves and fishes Jesus multiplied more than once, and the enormous amount of water turned into wine at Cana, and the impossibly large yield in the Parable of the Sower ("a hundredfold"), this episode again suggests the multiplicity and variety of those called and welcomed into the kingdom—but also that there is plenty for all.

In fact, the whole episode is a symbolic study of the church that Jesus intended: catching (fish), feeding (fish and bread), guiding (sheep). It also contains the clear rehabilitation of Peter from apostasy (*without* reparations) and the immediate conferral on him of the leadership of Jesus's community (like the father of the prodigal giving him not a penance but a party!). Like Jesus's tunic at Calvary, the net here is not torn apart.

What is so appealing about the scene is that, unlike most stories of that time, this one is so "thingy," so filled with concrete details, as Jesus as a father tells his sons, "Come, get your breakfast."

      Broke the bread. The lack of wine precludes a direct reference of this moment to a formal Eucharist. And yet, just as the multiplication of the loaves and fishes at this same lakeside and the encounter of two disciples with the risen Jesus on the way to Emmaus ("They knew him in the breaking of the bread" [Lk 24]) "resonate" with the Eucharist, so here too, despite any scholarly hesitations.

      Not one of them dared ask. In none of the resurrection scenes do any of those present unhesitatingly recognize Jesus. Such experiences were no more common then than now. They were befuddled because Jesus "wasn't the same." And yet he was. He was Jesus *transformed.* He was now, clearly, "the Lord."

      Fish/sheep. There is a fusion of two metaphors for Peter (and by extension all church leaders), nor should that cause conflict. The church is apostolic;

we are sent to harvest and gather but also to feed and care for, comfort, defend, guide.

↝ *Even if the others*. Earlier at the last supper (Mt 26:33), with typical bravado, Peter has sworn, "Even though all the others desert you, I will never desert you."

↝ *Love*. Some critics make much of the fact that the editor uses the word *agapan* for Jesus's first two inquiries about Peter's love but *philein* for the third. The connotations of *agapan* are like the medieval ideal of courtly love, a kind of purified awe, esteem, reverence, untainted by anything self-serving like lust or possessiveness. *Philein*, on the contrary, is down to earth: affection, warmth, fondness. Perhaps from some Platonic preference academic critics have for the unsullied, they suspect a kind of letdown in having Jesus's climactic question be about the love Simon Peter, the big-hearted fumbler. is so good at.

When the public sinner weeps on Jesus's feet and dries them with her hair, Jesus responds, to the shock of his host at his forgiving her: "Much is forgiven her because she has loved much" (Lk 7:47).

No matter how scrupulous the gospel editor might have been in his word choice, many less fastidious than the experts would prefer Christian love to mean something more spontaneous, less scrutinized, more heartfelt, less analytical.

↝ *Peter's restoration*. There is no single case in the Gospels where Jesus requires a sinner to beg forgiveness: the public sinner, the adulterous woman, the prodigal son. And not Simon Peter—despite the fact his sin was far more serious. He *apostatized* within an hour or two of the last supper, denied his friend and Lord with oaths too fierce to print in the Gospels. Nor was it a sin of witless abandon to passion in lust or anger. It happened three times in one night with time between to ponder. Nor was his denial to a soldier with a knife at his throat but to a brash *bystander*. It had even been *foretold* by Jesus at the supper.

～ *Peter's empowerment*. Earlier (Mt 16:18), Jesus changed Simon's name to Peter (Rocky) and told him he is to be the rock on whom Jesus founds his community. He has told the others (Mt 4:19) they will be fishers of men. But here he designates *only* Peter as the shepherd. It is interesting to ask why the final editor of the Fourth Gospel, writing twenty or thirty years *after* Peter's death, should single Peter out as a unique authority—if not to stress that the writer's contemporary church believed that Peter's power had devolved also onto his successor.

～ *Peter's death*. This inclusion is one more piece of evidence of the influence of later events on later treatments of the Jesus events. The writer knew Peter had ultimately sealed his declarations of his love with his death. In his final act Peter totally reversed his previous cowardice and went to crucifixion, refusing to deny not only his devotion to Jesus but his belief that Jesus had come back to life.

～ *Peter's position*. In this "last word" in the Gospel of John, Simon Peter stands out sharply from the others. But another insight in the concreteness of this episode indicates strongly that the Christian community is *not* focused on the next life but rather on this life.

Epilogue

Parable Lives

Every perfect life is a parable
invented by God.

—Simone Weil

At the outset, this book challenged what seems to
have become a taught and preached placebo Christianity, the brisk, sinewy challenges of Jesus *purged*
of unpleasant intrusions like loving our detestable
neighbor (Good Samaritan, Lk 10), peeling away
corrosive grudges (Unmerciful Servant, Mt 18), sur-
mounting natural reserve to stand up and be counted
(Persistent Widow, Lk 18). All well and good to accept
Jesus Christ as our personal savior as long as doing
so doesn't involve picking up the other end of his un-
wieldy cross every day.

Like the original parables—spoken and acted out—
these versions were intended to unsettle. Because that
seems as good a description as any to capture what the
words "the will of God for me" actually *mean*. Not
some invariant master plan, not a blueprint, not a play
script. Instead, a lifelong exercise in improvisation. So
every day we ought to get up and say, "OK, Dad. What
cha gonna throw at me today? I'm readier than I was
yesterday." Beats *Brave New World*.

The Father we share with Jesus seems to wait until our lives are bumping along just fine—and then
pounces. Like Kato ambushing Inspector Clouseau.
Why? One reason is quite likely that the God who
seems smitten with evolution has an aversion to complacency, to status quos. As the inspired prophet Bob
Dylan put it, "Whoever's not busy being born is busy

dying." The real cutoff point will come soon enough. A lot of Jesus's parables hinge on being caught napping. Not unseemly fear but surely at least *awareness* of the unpredictable certainty of our finitude. I've tried to make the dramatic shift from what we were *taught*: to fear being caught by death—or the end—befouled in sin to a more Jesus-like understanding that we begin to be at least aware of death finding us listless, bored, immobilized in neutral. "I have come that they may have *life*—and have it more *abundantly*!" (Jn 10:10).

Take some time with a notebook. Just brainstorm at random the peak moments of your life—the triumphs and the tragedies. Then go back and flesh them out with concrete specifics. Ponder each one slowly, like intuiting the meaning of the symbols in a dream. (Psst! It's not cheating to ask God to help.) In each of those happy and hapless moments, what message was God trying to get through to your understanding—a reworking of your certitudes you never would have accepted had it been delivered by some professor or homilist.

It would be a pity to miss the message of your own One-on-one parables.

"Whoever's not busy being born is busy dying."